Leadership Challenges for Servant Leaders

John J. Sullivan

Other books by John J. Sullivan

Servant First! Leadership for the New Millennium, Xulon Press, 2004

Seven Virtues, The Adventures of John Mouse, Xulon Press, 2010

Formatting Tips for Publishing a CreateSpace Book & Kindle Direct eBook, CreateSpace, 2012

Books in the series, Leadership Challenges for Servant Leaders:

My Betrayer is at Hand, CreateSpace, 2012

Details, Details, Details, CreateSpace, 2012

Truth Telling, CreateSpace, 2012

Severing the Ties That Bind, CreateSpace, 2012

Good News -- Bad News, CreateSpace, 2012

Eliminate Goal-Setting?, CreateSpace, 2012

Strategy and Plans, CreateSpace, 2012

Dedicated to leaders who
see themselves as servants first

For I know the plans that I have for you, declares the LORD, plans
for welfare and not for calamity to give you a future and a hope.
-- Jeremiah 29.11

Where there is no vision,
the people are unrestrained...
-- Proverbs 29:11

Do nothing from selfishness or empty conceit,
but with humility of mind regard one another
as more important than yourselves;
do not merely look out for your own personal interests,
but also for the interests of others.
--Philippians 2:3,4

To manage, one must lead.
--W. Edwards Deming

Preface

This book is the complete works in the series on leadership challenges for servant leaders. This book brings all of the individual monographs published separately together in one volume. The series addresses some of the most common leadership challenges in organizations today. Although the challenges are similar across organizations, the leadership styles which confront them are varied.

Leadership is leadership, whether one leads a small fellowship group or a large corporation, a squad or a corps, a team or an institution. What changes are the language (terms, acronyms) and the rules of engagement (how you interact with followers).

Interestingly, the more senior one becomes the more important are interpersonal relationships. This is counterintuitive at first glance but consider that as one leads larger and more complex organizations one becomes less and less an expert in what the organization does. The further one gets from "the product" the less one knows the product. Senior leaders become increasingly dependent upon followers who have the product expertise they lack; therefore the ability to build and maintain strong interpersonal relationships with core individuals within organizations is key to upper mobility and senior leader success.

This book is aimed at servant leaders or what Jim Collins calls Level 5 leaders[1]. This leadership model is best exemplified by the leadership style of Jesus of Nazareth who said He came to serve and not to be served. Leaders in industry, government, not-for-profit organizations and churches are discovering that the servant leader model is highly effective across organizational types.

---

[1] Collins, Jim, *Good to Great: Why Some Companies Make the Leap . . . and Others Don't*, HarperCollins, 2001

This upside-down leadership style puts the needs of followers above those of the leader, promotes teamwork, individual dignity and worth, and results in a synergy of purpose unachievable with the old leadership models. Its application in today's organizations creates an environment in which people freely choose to create, innovate, and strive for excellence.

I trust that you will be challenged by the discussion herein and would appreciate your feedback and lessons learned. Please contact the author at www.servantleaderministries.org.

Table of Contents

Introduction

What are the most common leadership challenges that leaders in every organization face? Are these challenges unique to one type of enterprise? Do leaders of for-profit companies face different challenges from those in the not-for-profit sector? I posed these questions to leaders in various types of organizations: for-profit companies, not-for-profit organizations, government, education, churches and parachurch organizations. The answers came back with regular similarity confirming my premise that most leadership challenges are not unique to one type of organization. Another truth was that we can learn from the experiences of leaders in organizations dissimilar to our own because of the one constant across all of the organizations: people. We are all dealing with people and regardless of the "product" you produce, leading people requires a certain set of skills and behaviors.

This book, then, addresses a common set of problems confronting leaders across the organizational spectrum. These, clearly, are not all the problems that leaders face but rather those issues that seem to occur in every type of organization. My goal has been to try to provide guidance for leaders who have a servant's heart toward their followers and who want to fashion their leadership style after the One who said that leaders should seek to serve rather than be served.

The first of these "challenges" is betrayal. Rather an odd way to start a book on leadership? you might say. Not really, since I doubt there is a leader out there who has not experienced this crushing experience. We will address three forms of betrayal and suggest a set of strategies for leaders to confront betrayal with total forgiveness.

1

John J. Sullivan

Next we turn to that persistent problem with many leaders: the tendency to micromanage. We address the reasons for micromanagement and how to overcome that insecurity, how to effectively delegate, and how to use teams in decision-making.

How much information should leaders make available to their employees or subordinates? Is it wise to restrict the flow of information on organizational performance? Are there advantages to sharing production and financial data across the organization? These and other issues of information sharing--truth telling--are discussed and a relatively new leadership approach known as open book management are introduced. This calls for blurring the lines between leader and followers and creating an environment of openness and accountability.

I was asked, how do I terminate a friend without humiliating him or making him an enemy? A better question might be: how do you let someone go where they are left with their dignity and you retain your integrity? Would you agree with me that most leaders don't do a good job of this? Severing The Ties That Bind will present a set of objective criteria to use when considering releasing an person, when to make the termination effective, and how to communicate this to the employee and the organization. Finally, we look at the impact on the remaining members of the organization and how to manage the inevitable questions and rumors that arise with every termination.

Good News -- Bad News examines another critical leadership function that most leaders don't do well--performance evaluation. We start by identifying the real purpose for performance evaluation, then move to the frequency of evaluation, how to measure performance, how to communicate the good, the bad, and the "other" and have the employee hear and understand what is being communicated. Finally, the setting for the discussion is examined.

Did W. Edwards Deming, the father of the Quality Revolution, really repudiate one of management guru Peter Drucker's most respected tools: Management by Objectives? Did he mean that goal-setting is counter-productive? If you don't have goals how will you measure performance? I argue that Deming's critique of MBO is widely misunderstood and that he taught that goals set by management without a complete understanding of the processes and systems under study will result in unrealistic goals leading to failure and disappointment. We examine the principles of MBO, how to construct SMART goals and the importance of the leader's attitude toward followers throughout the process.

We conclude our discussion of common leadership challenges with Strategy and Plans. Now here is something that every leader knows he or she should do, i.e., long range planning, but few do effectively. I describe a complete Strategic Assessment and Plan that may be adapted to any type of organization. This assessment and planning tool has four phases and ten steps and is summarized in Appendix A. It begins with an assessment of our current environments, both internally and externally. Next, we identify desired outcomes both in the short-term and long-term (goals and objectives). Third, we construct implementation plans to achieve our operational goals and strategic objectives. Finally, we develop methods for monitoring performance, analyzing feedback, reviewing and evaluating our plans.

Let's begin.......

John J. Sullivan

1

My Betrayer Is At Hand

Betrayal! Maybe you don't think of that as a significant leadership issue. I had not. Not until I asked a friend—the founder and leader of a large sport ministry—what were his top two or three leadership challenges? He responded immediately with "betrayal." Then as we were talking I began to think of the few times that a leader had betrayed me and how that had changed my life in significant ways. Does that mean that betrayal is a good thing? Obviously not, but it can result in positive changes to your attitude, faithfulness, and trust-level when you respond correctly to the betrayal.

Betrayal is destructive to any organization because it involves a breakdown in trust

Betrayal is destructive to any organization because it involves a breakdown in trust—the fundamental, root cause of failure of most organizations. Now that is a pretty bold statement! But my experience and research have shown me that when you dig down to the very bottom issue infecting failing or failed organization, you will find a breakdown in trust. That failure can be lack of trust in the leader, lack of trust in followers, lack of trust between co-workers, or all of the above.

Trust is essential to the healthy life of any organism, whether that is your family or the organization where you work.

John J. Sullivan

Over the last 10-15 years we've observed the growing popularity of executive ropes courses, outdoor adventure short courses and the like, all designed to develop trust and teamwork among leaders and co-workers. This is a recognition that without trust in one another there is no creativity, risk-taking, ingenuity, and growth. People must know that everyone else is doing their part, pulling their load. And without these, no modern organization can long survive.

To use a sports analogy, every member of the Boston Red Sox must have faith that each of their teammates is doing their job to the best of their ability if they have a chance to beat the New York Yankees. If even the right fielder (sorry, right fielders!) is daydreaming during the game, there is a chance that he will miss a critical fly ball at just the wrong moment. His teammates must trust that he is focused on the game and not on the fishing trip he has planned for next week. Or worse, they must trust that he is not betting against them to win the game. Each member of the team plays a critical role in the overall success of the franchise, including the management and front office. No one is more important than anyone else. Each person must have trust in their leaders and co-workers if the organization is to succeed.

Betrayal is a deliberate violation of trust. I will address three types of betrayal:

1. Betrayal of a follower by his leader;
2. Betrayal of a leader by his follower, or,
3. *Perceived* betrayal.

How does a follower react when his leader betrays him? Our human nature fights to control our emotions and we want to lash out at the betrayer. It takes a deliberate and willful attitude of trustfulness to overcome what our emotions are screaming at us to do.

Leadership Challenges for Servant Leaders

Maybe you remember the story… A young, obscure sheepherder is anointed to be the future king. He is called to minister to his country's king because of his musical skill. The king loves the young man and his music soothes his troubled spirit. Later, in a *mano y mano* fight the youth defeats the taunting braggart champion of his nation's sworn enemy and is elevated to a position of senior military leadership. Hearing the acclamations of the people for the young man, the king becomes suspicious of his loyalty. Overcome with jealousy, the king tries to kill the

On at least two occasions, the young man is in position to easily kill the king but he refuses

young man but he escapes from his hand. Others gather to the young man and he continues to elude the one who seeks to take his life. On at least two occasions, the young man is in position to easily kill the king but he refuses. When he declares this to the king, the king momentarily repents of his anger toward the young man but soon returns to his pursuit of him. After some time, the king is killed in battle. When the young man is told of his fate, he mourns the king. Later, he is anointed king.

This story of David and Saul, as recorded in the Old Testament Books of 1st and 2nd Samuel, provides us an excellent example of how to handle betrayal of a follower by his leader. Let's look at this from both perspectives: David's and Saul's. David did not conspire to become king. In fact when the prophet Samuel is sent by God to the family of Jesse of Bethlehem to anoint a new king over Israel, he too is surprised that the LORD would pick the youngest of eight sons to be the future king. David certainly had no ambition to be king as he tended his father's sheep. Can you image his bewilderment when Samuel declared that this young boy was the LORD's anointed?

David was selected by God to be the future king. However, throughout his relationship with Saul he remained steadfast and loyal to the king even as Saul came out with his army to destroy him. David must have wondered why GOD had chosen him and when he would become king but he never took matters into his own hand—even when he had the opportunity. He took no action, either overt or covert, to bring about his elevation. He relied on *God's* timing and *His* promises. Like all true servant leaders he operated out of a sense of calling (Ford 1991, Greenleaf 1991).

R. T. Kendall (2002) argues that King Saul's pursuit of David was really a blessing and the best thing that could have happened to David at the time. God was ensuring that David would be ready to wear the crown when his day came to be king. Martyn Lloyd-Jones has said, "The worst thing that can happen to a man is to succeed before he is ready." In Saul's betrayal of David, God did David a special favor by teaching David watchfulness, sensitivity to the Spirit and total forgiveness.

Saul, on the other hand, had lost his way. God had made him king over Israel, yet over time he wandered away from the LORD's will and became filled with suspicion and jealousy. Finally when he disobeyed the LORD's express will and took matters into his own hands, the prophet Samuel informed him that his kingdom would soon be ruled by another of God's choosing (1 Samuel 13:13,14). Saul saw David as a threat and sought to kill him. He had long forgotten to seek the LORD's will or to repent of his sins. He had sealed his own fate.

Fast-forward to a personal experience and the lessons learned from it. Following a tour as a fighter squadron commander, I had been assigned to a desk job at the Pentagon. Near the end of my 3-year tour there, I received a phone call from a friend who was the commanding officer of a Marine Corps air station where I had been stationed twice before. He had a intriguing offer to make: "Come down and be my executive officer for one year and then take over as commander of the station. After two years, you can move over and command the air group assigned at the station, too." (There were two colonel's billets on this installation: Station Commander and Air Group Commander.) I was caught completely off guard—and flattered—by this offer, as I had not even considered this as an option. I thought it doubtful that I would be given two choice back-to-back leadership positions but I asked, "What does the commanding general think of this?" I wanted to know if this was my friend's idea or had he the blessing of his boss—who would be the one who approved the assignment? He assured me that the general concurred.

When we hung up, I called the general, who had been my air group commander, and asked him if he approved of this plan. He assured me that he did. I thanked him for showing confidence in me and said that I would discuss it with my wife and that we would pray about it.

I waited a month while we prayed for God's will to be made known to us. During this time I received counsel, solicited and unsolicited, from friends and superiors—some said take the job and others advised against it. Over the course of the 30 days, we both felt a growing assurance that this was God's will for us and that I should accept the offer. So, a month later, I called my friend back and accepted.

I was about midway in my year as the executive officer when my friend, the commander, walked in to my office and announced, "I have some bad news for you." It seemed that the plan had changed and another man was to take over the air station and someone else was to command the air group. "That leaves you as the odd man out," he explained. I felt as if I had been physically assaulted with the air knocked out of me as he stood waiting for my response. Working hard to compose my face, I said that I would let him know what I wanted to do at the end of my year as XO.

My immediate response was: Whom can I call? What chips can I call in? Who can help turn this around? Why me? What have I done to deserve this? Not only had I been betrayed by my immediate boss who had recruited me but also by my former group commander. I though bitterly of the jobs that I turned down or did not pursue after being offered this one. I left the office soon after and drove home. Angry and hurt, I poured out the sordid story of betrayal to my wife. Her immediate reaction was, "Let's pray about this." She reminded me that we both felt strongly that it was the LORD's will that we accept this assignment. "If he wants us here, He will bring it about," she assured me. My human emotions wanted to lash out at this injustice but I surrendered to my wife's counsel and gave the matter into the hands of the LORD.

Some weeks later, I was told that the plans had changed, again, and that I was to become the station commander as originally promised. Oddly, this did not come as a surprise. For perhaps the first time, I experienced an indescribable peace knowing that God had me and my family's best interest at heart even (or especially) when things looked the bleakest. It was easy for me to say that I had surrendered my life and career to the LORD when things were going well and the way I had planned them. It was an entirely different matter when my carefully constructed plans were thrown into a wringer! I experienced a miracle by allowing God to do His work where I could not. Strangely, forgiving those who had betrayed me was not difficult.

> I experienced an indescribable peace knowing that God had me and my family's best interest at heart

What did I learn from this experience? Like David, I did not seek the position of leadership. Rather it was offered to me. Before accepting, I sought the LORD's will for my life through prayer, scripture and counsel. When I believed strongly that I understood the LORD's will—and that was confirmed by my wife—then I acted. When man schemed to change the plans of my Father, I leaned hard upon Him. I did not act disloyally toward my superiors, nor speak ill of them. I did not try to take matters into my own hands but allowed the LORD to demonstrate His faithfulness. I practiced total forgiveness toward those who had betrayed me. And He was faithful.

Leadership Challenges for Servant Leaders

You might ask, but what if the outcome had been different and you did not become the commander? How would I have reacted then? I trust that I would have had the faith to accept it as the LORD's will for my life and that He had something better in store for me.

How should a leader act when he discovers that one of his followers has betrayed him? Let's examine perhaps the most infamous betrayal of all time.

Over the course of three years the man had become one of his most trusted followers and even served as the chief financial officer. However, he had grown increasingly frustrated with his leader. He didn't understand why his leader wouldn't just come clean and assume his rightful place as a military conqueror. Why he wouldn't even use his obvious power to achieve the goals that this man and many of his friends expected of him! So perhaps to force his leader to act in accordance with his perception of the right course of action, he went to the leader's sworn enemies and offered to sell him out. Accepting blood money for his betrayal, he arranged for a secret sign to identify the leader to his enemies—a kiss. The next night he led armed guards to arrest his leader. Did he expect that his leader would strike out at the guards? Did he really intend that his leader would die as a result of his betrayal?

We will never know all the motives that drove Judas Iscariot to betray Jesus but we can examine Jesus' reaction to his betrayal (Matthew 26:14-25, 47-50). He did nothing. Although Jesus knew that Judas was going to betray Him (Matthew 26:21), when the time was at hand, he simply told him to do what he had to do and be quick about it (John 13:27). When Judas appeared in the night with armed guards to arrest Jesus and singled Him out by embracing Him, again Jesus did not lash out at

> Was Judas simply a pawn in God's great plan for the redemption of mankind?

11

his disloyal follower. Rather He "heaped burning coals on his head" (Romans 12:20) with a question, "Judas, are you betraying the Son of Man with a kiss?" (Luke 22:48) Even though Jesus had forgiven Judas his betrayal before it happened, Judas could not forgive himself. The sad story ended the next morning for a remorseful Judas when he hanged himself (Matthew 27:5).

Was Judas simply a pawn in God's great plan for the redemption of mankind? Did he think that he could force Jesus to be the conquering hero that Israel had been waiting for who would finally drive the occupying Romans from their land? Or was he just greedy? Maybe he was all of these. But our focus is on Jesus—how did He react to his betrayal and what can we learn from His actions?

When Jesus became aware of Judas' plan to betray Him, He:

1. Confronted him;
2. Took no action to prevent his betrayal;
3. When betrayed, He accepted his fate while remaining faithful to the Father; and,
4. Offered Judas total forgiveness.

Jesus knew there was a higher plan being worked out through the lives of imperfect men. Likewise when your follower betrays you there may be a higher plan that God has in mind for your life and work. By taking direct action you may actually be hindering that plan.

By His words and actions (a deliberate choice to *not* take retribution is an action) Jesus was living out His most difficult admonition to turn the other cheek, walk the second mile, love your enemies and to forgive those who harm you (Matthew 5: 39,41,44, 6:14). We may ask, surely He cannot expect *me* to do those things? After all, He was divine and how can mere mortal man measure up to His standard? Well, our answer can be found in the emphatic declaration of the 48th verse of Matthew 5: "Therefore you are to be **perfect**, as your heavenly Father is perfect (emphasis added)." Jesus doesn't cut us any slack! When He says something, He expects his followers to do it! And through the power of the Holy Spirit, we can.

He also expects us to forgive those who betray us. This is so important that Jesus included it in the prayer He taught His disciples (Matthew 6:12-15). We may have little trouble forgiving a small hurt caused by a follower, but what about a major act of betrayal? Yes, He expects us to forgive that too even if the betrayer is responsible for the deaths of our loved ones.

Corrie ten Boon survived the Holocaust, but her family did not. They were Dutch Christians imprisoned by the Nazis for hiding Jews in their home. She experienced the horrors of the genocide from the Ravensbrueck death camp and was the only member of her family to survive. Following the war, she became famous for her book, *The Hiding Place*, which shared the story of her family. She embarked on speaking engagements sharing her faith with thousands of people. One night at a church in Germany, she spoke about the reality of Christ's forgiveness. Afterwards a man came forward. "Fraulein Ten Boon, do you remember me?" Remember him! She had spent years trying to forget him! He was one of her guards at Ravensbrueck. "Yes, I remember you," she said coldly. With emotion choking him, the former Nazi asked, "Is it true that God can forgive me of all the horrible things I have done?" "Yes, God will forgive you as you give your life to him." "Oh, this is such good news," he said with tear-filled eyes. "Fraulein Ten Boon, will you forgive me?"

> Total forgiveness is a chosen privilege that requires a crossing over into the supernatural

Corrie stared at him and thought, "The question is not will I forgive you, but can I forgive you?" The answer was clear: NO! No, I cannot forgive him. I don't have that much love. Yet, she knew, for the sake of both of them, she must forgive him. So she prayed silently, "Lord, I cannot love this man. I cannot forgive him. Give me your love so that through you I can begin to forgive him so he and I can find the healing we both need." As she prayed, she felt a

13

sensation begin in her heart and flow through her hand as it touched his. Then she heard herself saying, "In the name of Jesus Christ, I forgive you" (Boom 1973).

Kendall (2002) argues that total forgiveness is a chosen privilege that requires a crossing over into the supernatural. It is a privilege to be like God and to pass forgiveness on to another. Jesus reminds His disciples: "But if you do not forgive men their sins, your Father will not forgive your sins" (Matthew 6:15). Therefore we have no excuse to hold hard feelings, pain, or hurt in our hearts over the betrayal of another. Nelson Mandela had been asked many times how he avoided bitterness after all those years in prison. He replied, "Bitterness only hurts oneself. If you hate, you will give them your heart and mind. Don't give those two things away" (Kendall 2002, 163). Jesus tell us the greater the hurt, the greater the blessing that will come with forgiveness (Matthew 5:11,12). We must stand on that promise.

What could be worse than betrayal by members of your own family? The story of a young man from the book of Genesis provides us with a fascinating account of betrayal, forgiveness, and redemption.

Joseph, the eleventh of twelve sons of Jacob and obviously a favorite of his father, was sold into slavery at the age of seventeen by his jealous brothers. Stolen from his home and his family, Joseph was eventually transported to Egypt and sold to one of Pharaoh's officials, Potiphar, the captain of the palace guard. Joseph quickly became a trusted and efficient servant and Potiphar soon put him in charge of his entire household and everything that he owned. "So he left in Joseph's care everything he had; with Joseph in charge, he did not concern himself with anything except the food he ate." (Genesis 39:6) Just when things were looking up for Joseph, the second major calamity in his life struck. Potiphar's wife tried to seduce him and when he refused she cried rape! Joseph's angry master had him thrown into prison.

Joseph's godly character and abilities soon came to the attention of the jailer. "(T)he LORD was with him; he showed him kindness and granted him favor in the eyes of the prison warden. So the warden put Joseph in charge of all those held in the prison, and he was made responsible for all that was done there. The warden paid no attention to anything under Joseph's care, because the LORD was with Joseph and gave him success in whatever he did" (Genesis 39:21-23).

> Nothing happens in any particular unless GOD's will is behind it, therefore you can rest in perfect confidence in Him.
> --Oswald Chambers

Here is Joseph again as a servant, or in this case as a prisoner, and again he is elevated to a position of leadership by others who recognize his innate ability to lead. What is starkly missing from this story is any grumbling or complaining on the part of Joseph. He accepted his fate as GOD's will for his life—at that time, and went about his duties as best he knew how.

Sometime later, Pharaoh's chief cupbearer and baker were implicated in a conspiracy against the king and thrown into the same prison with Joseph. When Joseph came to them the next morning, he found them dejected. The men related that they had both had bad dreams and did not know what they meant. Joseph correctly interpreted the dreams and his prophecy was fulfilled three days later. As Joseph had foretold, the cupbearer was restored to his position but the chief baker was hanged. Meanwhile, Joseph continued to languish in prison.

Two years later, Pharaoh had a dream that all the magicians and wise men of Egypt could not interpret. Suddenly the chief cupbearer remembered Joseph who was quickly summoned to Pharaoh's court. "'I had a dream, and no one can interpret it,' Pharaoh said. 'But I have heard it said of you that when you hear a dream you can interpret it.' 'I cannot do it,' Joseph replied to

Pharaoh, 'but God will give Pharaoh the answer he desires'"
(Genesis 40:15, 16). After hearing his dream, Joseph told Pharaoh
that God had showed him that there would be a severe famine in
the land following seven years of plenty. He went on to
recommend a course of action to prepare for the coming disaster.
Pharaoh was so impressed with Joseph's godly wisdom that he
immediately placed him in charge of "...the whole land of Egypt"
(Genesis 41:41).

Joseph did prepare Egypt for the famine that was to come as
he had prophesied. Two years into the famine, his brothers arrived
in Egypt seeking grain for their starving family and flocks. When
they presented themselves before Joseph, he recognized them but
they did not know him. Eventually, Joseph revealed himself to his
brothers with great emotion. Naturally, they were fearful that he
would punish them for the dreadful deed they had done to him
many years earlier, but Joseph assured them, "Now do not be
grieved or angry with yourselves, because you sold me here, for
GOD sent me before you to preserve life...Now therefore, it was not
you who sent me here, but GOD." (Genesis 45:5-8)

Joseph accepted his fate with complete trust in GOD
knowing that He always had his best interest at heart. Certainly
there were times when he must have questioned why GOD would
allow his circumstances but he never gave up hope that GOD did
have a plan for his life. After years of captivity and privation, he was
elevated to senior leadership and was able to save a nation, and his
family, from starvation. He did not take vengeance against his
brothers nor retaliate any way. Rather, he forgave them and
allowed GOD to work His way with his brothers.

Have you ever suspected that someone had betrayed your
confidence, or worse, was actively working for your downfall? How
many hours did you agonize over this perceived betrayal? How
many nights of lost sleep and days of productive work were
consumed with this fear? In the end did you discover that your
fears were groundless and that your imagination had simply been
running wild? I suspect that many of us have had these

experiences. They are wasteful and energy robbing. Our work, ministry, and family life all suffer as we fret over the perceived sins committed against us. Surely there must be a better way.

Jesus demonstrated how to deal with this type of conflict. It begins with identifying the extent of the disruption to our work, ministry and home life caused by the perceived conflict. If the conflict was incidental to the mission before Him He would ignore it and not make relatively minor events into major incidents. However, if the conflict was essential or unavoidable, He would directly confront it and then move on (Ford 1991).

We may apply this approach to the situation where we perceive someone has betrayed us. The question we must answer is: Is this (perceived betrayal) disruptive to the mission set before me? If the answer is no, then we are to put the issue behind us and move on. If the answer is yes, then we must confront the perceived betrayer. Do this carefully and prayerfully so as not to make the matter worse. Confront the individual you suspect of betrayal with the facts as you know them and ask directly if they have done what you suspect. If they deny any attempt to betray you, accept that and move on. If they admit the betrayal we are commanded to forgive them.

It is often the breakdown of trust that, like a cancer, eats the heart out of organizations

Trust is essential for people living or working together—whether in a family, a business, or a church. It is often the breakdown of trust that, like a cancer, eats the heart out of organizations. Betrayal is a deliberate breaking of trust and one of the most hurtful actions that one person can inflict upon another. This is especially true when it involves a loved one or close associate. We have examined three types of betrayal:

1. Betrayal of a follower by his leader;
2. Betrayal of a leader by his follower, or,

17

        3.   *Perceived* betrayal.

Even though the person doing, or suspected of doing, the betrayal is different in these situations our response should be the same. I believe these truths apply to every situation. When confronted with betrayal, we must always remember that:

        1.   The LORD has a plan for your life and it's a good plan (Jeremiah 29:11);

        2.   The LORD's will cannot be thwarted by man's plans (Romans 8:31);

        3.   Earnestly seek the LORD's will for your life (Psalm 105:4);

        4.   When betrayed by man, rely on the LORD's faithfulness to see His plans to fruition (Deuteronomy 7:9);

        5.   Totally forgive your betrayer and do not take retaliatory action, leave that to the Father (Deuteronomy 32:35), rather remain loyal;

        6.   Trust that God can work a miracle through the betrayal (2 Corinthians 12:9).

2

Details, Details, Details

To micromanage or not to micromanage, that is the question. With apologies to The Bard, this is an issue that many leaders struggle with. "Some managers love to sweat the small stuff," began an article in the Wall Street Journal (Sandberg, 2006). The same is true of leaders. But is this an appropriate behavior for a servant leader?

A servant leader assumes a position of trust with and toward his followers and works to develop each person to his full capacity. That requires the delegation of tasks and responsibilities, including leadership responsibilities, from the senior leader to subordinate leaders. Leaders who will not or cannot delegate are fundamentally insecure. They are fearful that a subordinate will make a mistake and make them look bad. They are convinced that no one can do the job as well as they can and so they hang on to the responsibility themselves. As a result, the work may get done but subordinate leaders are not developed and while the leader is failing at one of her primary functions, i.e., developing new leaders. Other symptoms of an over-controlling leader include: high turnover, lack of creativity and innovation, low morale, and restricted growth.

Leaders who will not or cannot delegate are fundamentally insecure

John J. Sullivan

Allowing someone else to take responsibility for a group of people and its function that you have been responsible for takes *confidence* in that person. By delegating that responsibility, you are saying, in effect, I *trust* you to carry on—and even improve upon—the work that I put my heart and soul into. This can be especially hard for someone who founds an enterprise and accounts for why many entrepreneurs struggle with growth in their organizations once they become larger than one person can successfully lead.

An enterprise will not long endure or grow where the leader will not delegate his responsibilities to others. And one of the important characteristics of a servant leader is his desire to develop his subordinate leaders to their full capability. One important way senior leaders do that is by delegation. This demonstrates that you not only trust the person to assume an important responsibility but that you are willing to allow them to fail. That takes confidence. A servant leader assumes that people will rise to the trust placed in them but is prepared to acknowledge failure when it comes—and it will. Servant leaders see failure as an opportunity to learn and to grow and are therefore not afraid of it.

> This demonstrates that you are willing to allow them to fail

As organizations grow leaders become *more* dependent upon their followers and subordinate leaders. A large organization—one in which the leader can no longer reach out and touch each part of the organization on a daily basis, and where she is no longer expert in every area—requires delegation of functions and responsibilities just to maintain status quo. However, growth demands that leaders allow others to use their creativity and ingenuity to improve upon and develop new and better products and processes.

The traditional, paternal, command and control leadership form has dominated most cultures up to our modern times. However, going back even to the time of Moses the single leader/decision-maker model had problems. After God had miraculously led the Israelites out of Egypt, their first battle was with the Amalekites. The following passage is a symbolic illustration of the value of shared leadership.

"And so it was, when Moses held up his hand, that Israel prevailed; and when he let down his hand, Amalek prevailed. But Moses' hands became heavy; so they took a stone and put it under him, and he sat on it. And Aaron and Hur supported his hands, one on one side, and the other on the other side; and his hands were steady until the going down of the sun." (Exodus 17:11, 12)

The Israelites went on to defeat the Amalekites and Moses learned an important lesson in leadership: *leaders need trusted followers to hold them up when the burden of leadership becomes too heavy.*

Not long after this encounter, Moses' father-in-law Jethro came to him in the wilderness returning his wife and two sons whom Moses had sent home during the plagues in Egypt. Moses was about to learn another valuable lesson in leadership.

And so it was on the next day that Moses sat to judge the people; and the people stood before Moses from morning until evening. When Moses' father-in-law saw him he said, "What is this thing that you are doing for the people? Why do you alone sit, and all the people stand before you from morning until evening?" And Moses said to his father-in-law, "Because the people come to me to inquire of God. When they have a difficulty, they come to me, and I judge between one and another; and I make known the statutes of God and His laws."

So Moses' father-in-law said to him, "The thing that you do is not good. Both you and these people who are with you will surely wear yourselves out. For this thing is too much for you; you are not able to perform it by yourself. Listen now to my voice; I will give you counsel and God will be with you: Stand before God for the people, so that you may bring the difficulties to God. And you shall teach them the statutes and the laws, and show them the way in which they must walk and the work they must do. Moreover you shall select from all the people able men, such as fear God, men of truth, hating covetousness; and place such over them to be rulers of thousands, rulers of hundreds, rulers of fifties, and rulers of tens. And let them judge the people at all times. Then it will be that every great matter they shall bring to you, but every small matter they themselves shall judge. So it will be easier for you, for they will bear the burden with you." (Exodus 18:13-22)

In their second year of wandering in the wilderness, Moses was continually beset by the complaints of the people. Finally, he cried out to the LORD, "I am not able to bear all these people along, because the burden is too heavy for me. If you treat me like this, please kill me here and now—if I have found favor in Your sight— and do not let me see my wretchedness!"

So the LORD said to Moses: "Gather to Me seventy men of the elders of Israel, whom you know to be the elders of the people and officers over them; bring them to the tabernacle of meeting, that they may stand there with you. Then I will come down and talk with you there. I will take of the Spirit that is upon you and will put the same upon them; and they shall bear the burden of the people with you, that you may not bear it yourself alone." (Numbers 11:14-17)

What other authority do we need than God himself who instructs Moses to share decision-making with the elders of the people? These passages illustrate that the single chief tradition has had recognized shortcomings long before the modern era. Even with a hierarchical structure, a single decision maker cannot hope to "hold his hands up alone." Following the pattern of Moses, leaders must share decision-making through delegation while reserving only the most important decisions to themselves.

In a small organization, the temptation is to delegate those functions that the leader doesn't especially like to do. And this may be appropriate where the leader recognizes that he does not have the aptitude for certain responsibilities. Even in large organizations, leaders tend to focus on those functions that they are familiar with. For example, if the CEO came up through the sales division, his natural interest will often be in that functional area. And that's okay as long as he doesn't try to run the sales staff from the front office.

Leaders should determine what are the responsibilities and functions that they and they alone must do and then delegate all other responsibilities. Some responsibilities are common across all organizations, e.g., evaluation of senior staff. There may be a few functions unique to the organization, e.g., administration of the Sacraments by the ordained pastor/priest. However, there are only a few responsibilities that the senior leader cannot delegate. Begin by setting down on paper all the tasks you do that require a decision. Then ask, is there a subordinate leader who can make these decisions? In most cases you will find that someone else in the organization can be delegated the responsibility.

Setting aside those responsibilities that only the senior leader can do, you must now determine *who* will be delegated all the others. This entails an assessment of the skills and abilities of subordinate staff and leaders. Matching responsibilities to skills will place people with oversight of functions that they enjoy and in which they have natural skills and abilities. But there are times when leaders want to develop new skills and abilities in subordinate leaders and will deliberately give them responsibility over an unfamiliar area in order to develop that individual for senior leadership.

Leaders must not only delegate the *responsibility* over a process or function but also *authority* and *accountability*

In order for delegation to succeed, leaders must not only delegate the *responsibility* over a process or function and its people but also *authority* and *accountability*. Responsibility to perform a task without the authority to call upon resources (people, time, money, training, equipment, etc.) to complete the task will invariably lead to its failure. Likewise, delegating responsibility and authority without

23

holding that person accountable for the successful completion of the task will likewise doom it to failure. Although the senior leader cannot delegate *ultimate* responsibility for a task (the Captain is responsible for *everything* that happens on his ship) he must be willing to allow others to take responsibility and even fail, occasionally, if new leaders are to be developed.

How can leaders be assured that their delegation will succeed? Although they cannot be guaranteed a 100% success rate with good accountability feedback leaders will be able to determine when delegated responsibilities are not achieving desired results and make corrections.

Senior leaders never fully relinquish responsibility over people and functions. Rather, through delegation they extend their own reach through other subordinate leaders while encouraging their creativity and ingenuity. This requires feedback systems that allow the senior leader to stay current of the state and progress within the delegated responsibility or function. Holding subordinate leaders accountable requires that they are fully supportive of the goals and objectives to be achieved.

> Senior leaders never fully relinquish responsibility over people and functions

Ideally, they would have been participants in goal development and in crafting the tactics used to reach them.

Choosing *how* the senior leader will receive feedback may be the most difficult part of delegation. This first requires determining what metric(s) will be chosen in order to determine whether we are achieving our goal. In order to do this, leaders must ask two questions, "What are we trying to achieve?" and "How will we measure it?" Usually, multiple metrics will be employed to ensure that our objective is being properly assessed.

Let's look at some examples. Productivity improvement based on number of units per worker per hour increase, often considered the simplest and most straight-forward metric, will only give a partial answer to the objective. We must also measure the impact upon quality. Without doing so leaders may find that although the *gross* number of units produced increased, the *net* number, after rejects and rework, may have actually declined.

> **Goal:** increase production by 10%
> **Primary metric:** number of widgets being produced in a given period per worker
> **Secondary metric:** number of rejects and rework

In production, increasing the number of widgets produced per worker or per hour is a common goal. However, without a secondary measure of the effect upon the quality level of the process, this goal may be counterproductive.

Objective goals are much easier to measure than *subjective* ones. How do you determine if your customers are happy with your product? What metric will show you the satisfaction level of your work force? How do you measure the level of expertise within your management staff? A common complaint from people who leave one church for another is, "I wasn't being fed there." How does the pastor determine if the needs of his members are being met?

While the manufacturing sector may rely, at least partially, on objective metrics, the service sector must find ways of measuring feelings and impressions. This is a difficult task and one that takes time and experimentation. It begins with clearly defining *what* it is we want to measure. Once we determine the *what*, we then must search for *how* we can determine our progress. Don't be discouraged if

Don't be discouraged if the metric you choose turns out to be ineffective

the metric you choose turns out to be ineffective. Try another metric, or set of metrics, until you find what measurement gives you true feedback on the state of your objective.

>**Goal:** increase knowledge of technicians in emerging technologies
>**Primary metric:** end-of-course testing results
>**Secondary metric:** number of new products developed using emerging technologies

When determining metrics for measuring effectiveness of training, the temptation is to simply add up the number of hours, classes, or seminars attended. But just as having longer meetings does not mean that those meetings are more effective, *attending* training does not mean that the training was effective. What we want to measure are the *results* of training. Testing results can give us an indication of what was learned, but only secondarily. What we really want to measure is *how* the training was *applied*. What is our return on investment in training?

>**Goal:** provide for emerging needs of single-parent families within the congregation
>**Primary metric:** number of new single-parent families who join the church
>**Secondary metrics:**
>1. Quarterly satisfaction survey results
>2. Retention level of current single-parent families
>3. Personal interviews

Subjective feedback is often gathered through surveys, focus groups, and interviews. And there is nothing wrong with that form of metric provided we understand the limitations inherent in such instruments. However, they cannot be the only metrics. In the example cited above, the *real* indicator of program effectiveness in organizations where people are essentially volunteers—they are free to come or go—is retention and new members added to the target group.

One of the results of the "Quality Revolution" of the last 25 years has been the use of teams, both in the for-profit and not-for-profit workplace. American quality pioneers W. Edwards Deming, Joseph Juran, and others argued for a participatory form of management that drew on every employee's knowledge and abilities beginning in the late 1940's (Walton, 1990). Unfortunately for American industry, few leaders in this country heeded their counsel. However, leaders in Japan did and it wasn't until the early 1980's when Japanese industry was enjoying an ever-increasing market share, particularly in automobiles, that American business leaders began to pay attention. One of the keys to Japanese success seemed to be the use of teams of employees to solve problems, streamline processes, and overcome obstacles. As American industry began to experiment with the use of teams, many realized great success and the word spread. Within ten years, one would be hard-pressed to find a successful business that did **not** use teams in some way to increase efficiency and reduce costs.

The not-for-profit segment had already been using teams ("committees") for years as they depended largely on volunteers to do much of the work of their organizations. The focus on teams in industry brought a refinement in strategy and discipline to team functioning with organizations dedicated to training leaders and team members on how to function more effectively. Companies like Joiner Associates, Inc., were created and specialized in team training while publishing books on team concepts, roles and tools (Scholtes, Joiner, and Streibel, 1996).

Today, teams are "just the way we do business" in most successful organizations. However, the latitude given teams in decision-making is wide and varies from organization to organization. One entrepreneur who recognized that he could not handle the booming growth of his company and the demands of leadership alone is George Lopez. Dr. Lopez, an internist, founded

ICU Medical, Inc. in 1984. By the early 1990's, the company had about $10 million in annual revenue and was preparing for a public offering. Demand for the company's Clave product, used in connecting a patient's IV systems, was skyrocketing. Dr. Lopez needed to figure out how to ramp up production. The company had fewer than 100 employees but was expanding rapidly while he was still making most of the decisions.

Then he had an epiphany came while watching his son play hockey. The opposing team had a star, but his son's team ganged up on him and they won. "The team was better than one player," said Lopez. He decided that if his company was going to become what he hoped it could, he needed to learn to delegate decision-making to teams of people. This conclusion was not met with universal favor and some of his senior executives quit. Undeterred, Dr. Lopez put the new system in place and told employees to form teams to look for ways to boost production. Initially, the team effort failed. With no leaders, and no rules, "nothing was getting done, except people were spending a lot of time talking," said Lopez. After struggling for about 18 months, he decided to allow teams to elect their leaders. This brought a vast improvement in team effectiveness. In 1995, he hired a specialist to help define the structure and "rules of engagement" for teams. At the same time, they started paying teams rewards for cost/time-saving improvements.

The biggest difference between teams at ICU and most organizations is that the CEO has not vetoed a single team decision!

It worked, and employees began to embrace teams. Today, twelve to fifteen teams finish projects each quarter often meeting weekly.

The biggest difference between teams at ICU and most organizations is that the CEO has not vetoed a single team decision! Although he retains the right to nix decisions, Dr. Lopez said that for teams to work, "employees need to feel they have authority." A veto would "really have to be worth it," and the team decision would have to be putting the company "on a pathway to destruction." He has bitten his lip and never vetoed a team decision even when he disagreed with it. An example was a team that recommended instituting a 401(k) plan over the objections of senior executives and Lopez' concerns over the cost. He now concedes that the plan has helped in retaining employees (White, 2007).

To summarize, successful delegation requires not only assigning the responsibility for a function and its people to a subordinate leader but also the authority to call upon resources. Those leaders delegated responsibility must then be held accountable for the results they achieve. Delegation requires two-way trust and the willingness to allow people to fail while seeing this as an opportunity to grow. Holding leaders accountable requires first determining *what* will be measured and then *how* will effectiveness be measured. That usually requires multiple metrics and the willingness to frequently reevaluate them.

Large and complex organizations cannot function long with non-delegating leaders and small organizations that wish to grow will not do so unless leaders learn to delegate. Servant leaders recognize that one of their primary functions is to develop other servant leaders. They achieve this by investing in others, through their personal example, and by delegation. As a result, innovative organizations are created, grow and thrive.

John J. Sullivan

3

Truth Telling

The question from a senior human resources manager was, "How much do you tell?" How much information do you give your people about the organization? Is it better to withhold certain data from those who do not have a "need to know?" In most companies, and even not-for-profits, the answers to those questions would be "Not much," and "Yes!" But does this make sense and is it the best way for a servant leader to run an organization? Some leaders have taken another approach.

Jack Stack was 19 year old when he got his first real job at International Harvester. He was amazed at how dishonest people in the company were—even senior leaders. His job was to talk to production managers around the country and try to balance the supply of parts for the equipment they built. If one plant was running short of components used in production, he would look for another plant that had a surplus. Little did he know that there was an unwritten law among plant managers that you never told the truth. Why should you risk shutting down your assembly line by shipping components somewhere else? In his youthful naiveté, he always gave honest answers. Over time, more and more

Little did he know that there was an unwritten law among plant managers that you never told the truth

31

senior leaders would call him when they needed an honest answer. His visibility within the organization continued to increase simply because he told the truth (Muoio, 2007)!

A little over ten years later and now in middle management, Stack was sent to Springfield, MO, to shut down an ailing plant. Arriving at the plant, he faced a demoralized workforce on the verge of a union-organizing election. Somehow, he was able to rally the workers, stave off the union, and save the plant. Four years later, he negotiated the leveraged buyout of the division and built it into the star of its industry using a "unique" approach to leadership—telling the truth (Burlingham, 1989)! After a few rough start up years, Springfield Remanufacturing Company grew from $16 million in sales to more than $160 million. SRC has been recognized by Inc. Magazine as "one of America's most competitive small companies." The company has received both the National Business Ethics Award and the Business Enterprise Trust Award and was selected as one of the Top 100 Companies to Work For in America.

> This demonstrates that you are willing to allow them to fail

This may work for Jack Stack but will it work elsewhere? According to John Case (2004), author of two books on what he termed "open-book management," there are over 1,000 companies that practice this business model. A study by the National Center for Employee Ownership and Inc. Magazine found that open-book companies grew faster than their competitors while using resources more efficiently ("Open-Book Management and Corporate Performance," 2002).

Perhaps the greatest barrier to implementing OBM is cultural. In most organizations, employees (or team members, associates, etc.) typically view themselves as hired hands. People in open-book organizations have a different view. They see themselves as partners in the business who are concerned not just about doing their own jobs but with the business objectives of the organization (Case, 1998). OBM requires a change from the traditional top-down leadership style ingrained in most organizations. It means blurring the lines between leader and followers and creating an environment of openness and accountability ("The Case for Open-Book Management," 2004).

Open-book management describes a leadership style where financial and performance information is openly shared with all employees. It involves educating everyone about the organization's **It includes significant and timely rewards based on performance** business and exchanging information among them to support their active involvement as responsible business partners. It includes significant and timely rewards based on performance (Barkman, 1997). The organization must incorporate three principles which form the building blocks of an OBM system. First, you have to create a *transparent* company. That means that everyone, not just those at the top, sees and understands the real numbers. These are those critical metrics (both operational and financial) that are used to run the organization and gauge its performance. Second, you need a system of *joint accountability* where everyone is held accountable for their part in the organization's performance. And, third, you must give people a *stake in success* as well as pay them for their time. That means establishing a healthy bonus plan and usually an employee stock ownership plan (ESOP) (Case, 1989).

With these principles in mind, let's examine the five elements of a success OBM system. They are:

1. Leadership
2. Education
3. Information
4. Involvement
5. Rewards

John J. Sullivan

Open-book management requires a certain personal **leadership** philosophy. And it does require a philosophical change to the command and control leadership style of Frederick Winslow Taylor, the father of Scientific Management. During the Industrial Revolution at the turn of the 20th century, Taylor taught—and most organizations still practice—that people in the lower ranks of an organization should do as they were told by those at the top who knew best. OBM takes a very different approach which is as much a matter of the heart as it is of the mind (Barkman, 1997). A leader must be eager to share information, decision making, and wealth with his "partners" in the organization. People must have the real numbers about an organization's financial performance to achieve credibility and motivation. They must also have the opportunity to make a difference in a significant way and to share monetarily in the success of the organization.

Education means training and developing the knowledge and skills of people to do everything their jobs require. It also means understanding the business (mission) context within which their work is done. Everyone's job becomes larger because each person must understand how the organization operates financially and how they can affect financial results.

Information is widely shared across the organization. In order to understand the key financial metrics that determine success or failure of any organization, people must be both informed and educated. This is the defining element of OBM. Key financial and operating measures are carefully defined, measured, and intensely managed by all employees to produce results. The "critical number" may be different for every organization and will change over time. It represents a prime indicator of profitability or success. Discovering the critical number is a key component of an open-book organization. Once you determine your critical number, then a "scoreboard" is developed that brings together all the numbers needed to calculate the critical number (Stack, 1994). Instead of trying to satisfy manager's needs for information, OBM stresses the people have information so they can make decisions and respond to changes as needed.

Involvement means using problem-solving teams and natural work teams across the organization to harness the creativity and ingenuity of people to produce high level results. People are challenged each day to take action and make a difference for organizational success.

Rewards come from having a personal stake in the success of the organization. Educated and informed people who are deeply involved with organizational success will produce results when they see themselves as partners and are treated accordingly. When the organization does well, everyone enjoys a piece of the pie not just the senior leaders/owners. Rewards are linked directly to the critical numbers, both operational and financial (Barkman, 1997).

Is this approach compatible with servant leadership? The answer should be obvious---YES! Remember young Jack Stack's key to success? He told the truth. And because he told the truth he developed a reputation as a man of integrity—someone who could be trusted to tell all the facts "with the bark on." This led to opportunities which resulted in tremendous financial and personal success for Jack and the people of his companies. Modern cynicism among people across many cultures has created a distrust of authority whether in government, business, or the church. OBM aligns with servant leadership because it is founded on trust— between the leader and his followers. Trust is the cornerstone of a winning workplace and a servant-led organization. The leader sees his job as providing the resources so that people can achieve their highest levels of satisfaction and performance. He sees them as

> Trust is the cornerstone of a winning workplace and a servant-led organization

partners not as workers. Given that context, why would you *not* share detailed financial and production data with the people who are producing your products or services?

OBM creates a sense of ownership in the enterprise common to servant-led organizations. When describing the level of participation in the vision and mission of an organization, people will fall somewhere on a continuum between *enrolled* and *committed*. Being enrolled means that I do what is required on the job—nothing more, nothing less. I generally show up on time and leave right at quitting time. I contribute nothing to improving the workplace since it is not part of my job description. If the enterprise fails, I simply move on to another. Contrasted with this job-related attitude is the committed person. She is excited about her work and sees it as a challenge every day. Most days she can't wait to get to work and she often arrives early or stays late. She frequently works at home on the weekends on her own time. She is constantly thinking of ways to make her work, and the work of others, more efficient and more productive. She is actively looking for ways to cut cost, reduce waste and improve quality. She works hard to help make the organization successful and profitable. She thinks like an owner. Moving people from enrollment to commitment is fundamental to a servant-led organization. It is likewise the product of an open-book management enterprise.

Open-book management, like servant leadership, is as much a matter of the heart as it is of the mind. It describes an upside down leadership paradigm where the leader serves the people in order for them to achieve their highest level of performance and satisfaction. When people are truly loved, encouraged, and treated with dignity and respect, personal and organizational success follows.

Don Barkman (1997) summarizes the advantages of OBM:

1. Solid financial performance of the business.
2. Improved security for the firm and its members.
3. Increased satisfaction with work.

4.   Substantial   and   sustainable   personal compensation and wealth building.

These are certainly legitimate goals for a servant leader, as well. Comparing the leadership traits of Jesus, the model for a servant leader, and OBM, we see that the traits of a servant leader and one practicing open-book management are nearly identical (see Figure 1).

Servant Leadership vs. Open-Book Management

Trait	Servant Leadership	OBM
Compassion	X	
Humility	X	X
Integrity	X	X
Trustworthy	X	X
Knowledge	X	X
Commitment	X	X
Empowerment	X	X
Motivator	X	X
Reconciler	X	X

FIGURE 1

A   leader   who   practices   open-book   management demonstrates humility by admitting his fallibility. He does not seek to acquire power over others by selectively disclosing information. He acknowledges that he does not have answers to all the problems and challenges facing the organization. He can be trusted to tell the truth and to keep a confidence. He has excellent knowledge about the organization's mission and its products and services but continually seeks to increase his knowledge base. He is committed to the long-term success of the organization above his own personal success. He empowers others to take ownership of their processes by first enabling them with training and other educational resources. He motivates himself and others through an intrinsic sense of satisfaction in doing a job well and by sharing in the earned wealth of the enterprise. He is a reconciler of differing views working to achieve a synergy of purpose. He is a man of integrity and a model for others. (One may argue that an OBM leader also demonstrates compassion toward those he leads—and I would not disagree.)[2]

Finally, the best test of a servant leader is whether he develops those around him into servant leaders, too (Greenleaf, 1991). That is the natural outfall of an OBM philosophy combined with a servant's heart. Jack Stack put it this way, "... we give people a tremendous lesson in entrepreneurship. After you've spent a year or two here, you walk away with a lifetime of lessons in running a business—your *own* business" (Burlingham, 1989). I believe that a servant-led organization will embrace a philosophy of openness across the organization recognizing the dignity and worth of each individual and valuing their contribution to the success of the organization. Those organizations that have embraced such a philosophy have enjoyed the rewards of material and spiritual satisfaction that comes with meaningful work well done.

How much do you tell? Tell it all!

---

[2] For a complete description of the leadership traits of Jesus, see the author's book, *Servant First! Leadership for the New Millennium* (2004)

4

Severing The Ties That Bind

A friend of mine recently asked for advice on how to terminate a friend who worked for him without humiliating him. This is one of the toughest tasks for any leader whether or not it involves a friend. Involuntarily releasing an employee (termination) often has a profound impact upon the individual (self-identity, self-worth), his family, church, neighborhood, schools, etc. Therefore, it should never be taken lightly. In my experience, most leaders don't do a good job of this—be it a secular or Christian organization. However, there are times when a leader has to let someone go from their organization. This *can* be done with dignity and grace but it takes some planning.

> Most leaders don't do a good job of this— terminating employees

There are four questions that leaders need to ask themselves before they approach an employee to be terminated:

1. *Why* are we terminating this person?
2. *When* should this be effective?
3. *How* do we inform the employee?
4. *What* do we do afterwards?

Are there good reasons for terminating a person's employment? Of course there are. In general, termination is justified when an employee demonstrates:

1. Gross incompetence and a refusal to learn;
2. Immoral, illegal or unethical behavior;
3. Flagrant disloyalty.

However, most decisions on termination are not so straightforward. More likely the reason will fall into one of these categories:

1. The function or process they perform is no longer required (functional obsolescence), e.g., work moved offshore, process outsourced, several small schools combined into one large school, etc.
2. They no longer possess the necessary skills (skill obsolescence).
3. Reduction in size of the workforce (RIF) due to downsizing, focus on core competencies, merger, technological efficiencies, etc.
4. Change of mission/products/service (mission obsolescence).
5. Repeated violations of work rules (discipline).
6. Failure to meet goals (performance).

Some of these reasons are beyond the control of the employee (functional obsolescence, RIF, mission obsolescence). Skill obsolescence *may* be the employee's fault, but as Peter Drucker (2001) reminds us people today must be continually learning new skills in order to remain effective. Part of the blame could also rest with leadership if the individual was not given an *opportunity* to acquire new skills. When discipline problems are the cause for termination, it is usually pretty straightforward: i.e., repeated violation of work rules will result in termination. That leaves us with failure to meet goals (performance). This is where many leaders stumble.

When my friend contacted me, my response began this way, "I assume that you have already counseled this person over a period of time about his performance, set mutually-agreed upon goals, provided coaching and advice on achieving those goals, and documented the whole process." (See Chapter 5 Good News-- Bad News on performance evaluation for an explanation of the entire process.) Terminating an employee's employment due to poor performance should never be considered unless leaders have followed the steps outlined above. However, when leaders have worked with the employee over a period of time and their performance has not risen to acceptable levels, then, perhaps, termination is justified. In fact you are probably helping the individual by letting him go since it has become clear that he will not be successful if he remains.

> You are probably helping the individual by letting him go since he will not be successful if he remains

An alternative to termination should be considered when possible. Is this person better suited for another job within the organization? Would his skills be better utilized in another function? Are there physical or mental/emotional limitations that are hindering this person from being successful in this assignment? Leaders should consider lateral movement of employees who are fully committed to the vision, mission, and values of the organization but who lack competency in their current position. This is always preferable to termination.

Jack Stack, president and CEO of Springfield Remanufacturing Corporation, takes this approach. He says his purpose is to "...put the right people in the right jobs. I want to understand their strengths and weaknesses so I can match them with opportunities they're capable of handling" (Stack, 1997).

If the individual cannot be retained in the organization, another alternative is to ask the employee to resign. This allows the employee to receive a "clean" record from the organization and is usually more favorably received. It also permits the individual to retain a certain sense of dignity, which is preferable to termination and the perceived loss of dignity.

When leaders have exhausted all other opportunities, termination may be appropriate where it is in the **best long-term interest of the organization**. That has to be the bottom line reason: the health of the organization (and all of its people) requires it. A servant leader always puts the long-term success of the organization above his own even when that requires him to perform unpleasant tasks such as this.

When to make the termination effective will depend upon several factors unique to each situation. What are the contractual considerations? How much notice is required to terminate employment? Two weeks to 30 days is common but may be more depending upon the contract. Is there a penalty for early termination of a long-term contract? Cost is an important factor so if the cost to retain the employee (in opportunity lost, substandard production, low morale) until the expiration of their contract exceeds the cost to terminate then you would not want to terminate and accept the penalty.

Not renewing an annual contact is a much easier option than early termination. However, good leaders will have followed the model for performance evaluation and not renewing the contract should come as no surprise to the employee. Terminating a contract early is always difficult emotionally for the employee but also for the leader and should only be done when the good of the organization demands it.

Jim McCann, president of 1-800-FLOWERS, sought out the advice of then-General Electric CEO Jack Welch about how to terminate a senior executive in his company who was also a friend. After McCann described his situation, Welch responded, "When was the last time anyone said, 'I wish I had waited six months longer to fire that guy'? McCann concludes, "Always err on the side of speed" (Muoio, 2007).

Facing an employee that you intend to terminate is never easy. Good leaders accept this responsibility as part of their jobs although no one enjoys it. Informing an employee that they are being released from their job should usually be done by the direct supervisor, assuming this is the person who completes the employee's performance evaluation. If the next person up in the chain of command does the actual performance evaluation, then both the direct supervisor and this leader should inform the employee.

The meeting with the employee should be private and only the direct supervisor and his boss (if needed as described above) should be present along with the employee. Leaders should be very specific as to why the employee is being terminated. Provided you have done a good job of documenting the employee's performance and failure to achieve agreed upon goals, this discussion should surprise no one. Termination must be based on objective not subjective data. Leaders should avoid even the appearance of attacking the individual and limit criticism to performance issues rather than personal issues.

Servant leaders who truly care about their employees will offer to help the individual find other employment. Tell the individual exactly what you are willing to do and say with regard to reference inquiries from potential future employers. If you do not believe you can give this person a favorable reference, tell him so. If you believe that this person's skills and abilities would be better utilized in another occupation, advise him of that and encourage him to look in that field. Perhaps additional training is required in order to be competitive in another field. Advise the employee of this and make suggestions as to how to obtain this training.

Termination must be based on objective data

The employee should be given a reasonable amount of time to close out his affairs with you. Although two weeks notice is common, thirty days is even better. What are your expectations during this period? Be very specific as to what you expect over the last few days of employment. Will you give the employee time off to look for another job? If so, tell him and how much time you will allow. What tasks do you want completed before the employee leaves? Outline those in the interview and ensure that they are finished. If the employee has company equipment, uniforms or tools, set up a time when these will be inventoried and returned.

Who needs to be informed of the termination? The appropriate human resources personnel need to be informed ahead of time that you intend to terminate an employee. They should be instructed to remain quiet about the termination until it is made public. No one wants to read in the paper that they have been "fired" before even they know. Unfortunately this happens far too often especially with high profile persons.

Following the termination interview the employee should be allowed to leave the premises and inform his family before any public announcement is made. If the person is a high profile, well-known individual a press release may be appropriate the following day. This should be carefully worded and reviewed by knowledgeable personnel (e.g., legal counsel) to insure that it does not cause embarrassment to the individual, his family or make the organization liable in any way for future damages.

When someone is terminated there will always be questions, rumors as to why they were let go (most of which will be wrong), and other disruptions to the normal work schedule. The best way to address this is to call together the person's co-workers and inform them of the termination. This should be done the day following the meeting with the employee to allow him time to inform his family and closest friends. The leader who actually informed him of his termination should also be the one to inform his co-workers. If the immediate supervisor and his boss were both involved, then both should attend the meeting.

Leadership Challenges for Servant Leaders

The announcement to co-workers should be limited to an explanation of the termination and its effective date. For example: "Mr. Jones has resigned effective (date) or Mr. Jones will no longer be working here effective (date)." Explain that the resignation has nothing to do with Mr. Jones personally and that you wish him the best for the future. If pressed, the most you should say is that the issue is performance-related and a private personnel issue so you cannot say more.

Releasing an employee who has not been performing up to goals and expectations will not come as a surprise to his co-workers. In fact, some may even be pleased that their leaders recognized substandard performance and took action. In an open organization where there is good communication between the leaders and followers, everyone knows who is pulling their weight and who is not. Therefore, leaders send a strong message by removing those non-productive people from the organization. This should not be a threat to strong performers. Rather, it should encourage them.

> In an open organization where there is good communication everyone knows who is pulling their weight and who is not

Now comes the task of replacing the individual. Having co-workers involved in the final selection process demonstrates that leaders trust the employees and value their input. Co-workers are much more receptive to new employees that they have had a hand in selecting and the new employee will be more quickly socialized into the organizational culture.

Terminating an employee is one of the toughest decisions any leader has to face. However, a servant-first leader will make this decision and carry it out with dignity and respect for the individual by putting the overall welfare of the organization first. In the process you have probably done this individual a favor. Although it may not seem like it at the time, this could turn out to be the best thing for the person involved as well as the organization.

5

Good News - Bad News

Why do performance evaluation? What purpose does it serve? How often should leaders evaluate the performance of subordinates? How should they obtain performance information to make the evaluation?   What method should they use to discriminate between different people's performance? How does the leader tell people bad news without destroying their egos? Aren't most performance evaluations meaningless in terms of true "evaluation?" Let's take these questions one at a time.

Why do performance evaluation? Performance evaluation can be a powerful tool for leaders to help people become more productive, efficient, and effective. In short, their main purpose must be to help people grow. But they must be done right or they will do more harm than good. Jack Stack, president and CEO of Springfield Remanufacturing Corporation, agrees that, "...the typical annual–review process...creates divisions, undermines morale, makes people angry, jealous, and cynical. It unleashes a whole lot of negative energy and the organization gets nothing in return" (Stack, 1997).   Many people facing the annual performance evaluation are filled with fear and trembling especially when the evaluation is the first and only time they have received performance feedback during the year. Add that lack of feedback to a coupling of the performance evaluation with future pay and promotion, and people are often terrorized by the thought of the interview. Most

47

leaders do not go to the extremes that Admiral Hyman Rickover, the father of the U.S. nuclear Navy, was famous for (more on that later) but suffice to say that the experience is often an unpleasant one for most people, and this includes leaders.

Fear of the interview sometimes leads to aberrant behavior on the part of the person being interviewed manifested by lying, exaggeration, blame displacement, or simply tuning out. Under these conditions, no learning takes place and future growth is stymied.

Performance evaluation should be for the purpose of helping people perform at a higher level. For the servant leader it should be a primary function of helping people to reach their full potential and true job satisfaction. It should involve measurement of goal achievement against previously agreed upon objectives and metrics. Where goals were not attained, we ask why not? Where they were achieved, we ask why? Was it due to what we did, did not do, or just luck? The answer to these questions will determine what changes, if any, we need to make to processes. Where goals were not achieved, leaders should ask the person being evaluated to explain the cause. Deming reminds us that 85% of the time (he later changed it to 96%) problems are due to the process and not the person (Deming, 1986). Leaders are responsible for the processes. Therefore, leaders must determine what tools or process changes are required to improve performance. For example, several years ago a salesman told me of his frustration to achieve ever increasing goals imposed by his supervisor while he continued to deny him use of a cell phone. He explained that he could use his time much more efficiently with a cell phone to insure that his contacts were available when he called on them.

> Performance evaluation should be for the purpose of helping people perform at a higher level

Determining *what* to evaluate is the first step in creating an effective performance evaluation. Are we going to evaluate *traits* (viz. stable aspects of people, closely related to personality), *behavior* (viz. what people actually do on the job), or *results* (viz. what people accomplish) (DuBrin, 2003). In most cases the best performance appraisal systems will rely mainly on evaluating results as these can be done objectively. The essential job functions to be measured must come from the tasks, duties, and responsibilities defined in the person's job description. Performance standards should be included in the job description which clearly states what performance is considered satisfactory in each area of the job (Mathis and Jackson, 1999). Evaluating a person on duties that are not part of the job description is not valid. Therefore, it is incumbent upon leaders to periodically review their employee's job descriptions to ensure that as duties change over time, these are reflected in their job descriptions.

True "performance evaluation" should happen every day, assuming leaders have daily contact with their people. If contact is less frequent, performance evaluation should occur whenever contact is made with the person. This informal feedback can be as simple as a compliment or correction on job performance yet is a powerful tool to encourage increased productivity. Daily, weekly, monthly, and quarterly goals may obviate the need for an annual review. The first time a person learns that his performance is not meeting goals should not be at the annual review. With short interval goals, each person knows exactly where they stand throughout the year.

It is virtually impossible for leaders to truly observe any employee's overall performance over a period of time

It is virtually impossible for leaders—with the possible exception of very small businesses—to truly observe any employee's overall performance over a period of time. Therefore, relying only on your own observations will tell just part of the story. A too common method is the "manager's notebook" where critical incidents are recorded (usually only the "bad" occurrences) and then used to form the evaluation. This method does not take into account a person's overall performance day-to-day and focuses on exceptions to behavior. It is as faulty as using varying standards to evaluate different people, applying greater weight to recent occurrences, or the "halo effect." This rater error is present when the leader rates the employee high or low on all items because of one characteristic (e.g., friendly, funny, or personable) (Mathis and Jackson, 1999).

How, then, is the leader to obtain a true picture of performance? Objective goal measurement is one way. Another is to obtain input, albeit often subjective, from several different sources. This is commonly called a "360 degree appraisal." It means that you get input from peers, suppliers, customers and even the employee herself before forming the evaluation. Granted, this is time-consuming and perhaps expensive, but it allows the leader to see what others perceive as the true performance of an employee. When reviewing the input from multiple sources, leaders should try to form an overall picture of the person's performance rather than focus on specifics within an externally obtained evaluation realizing that some distortion of performance is common.

A senior leader of a large multi-national corporation once told me that before he visits his senior managers around the world, he first visits their major customers and asks for an evaluation of the performance of the local office. He said this helps him to "cut through the hype" when determining the effectiveness of his outlying staff.

Some organizations require leaders to directly compare the performance of their employees against one another (Mathis and Jackson, 1999). These ranking and forced distribution methods are artificial and often arbitrary. Ranking people from highest to lowest or within a certain category to achieve the classic bell curve is not helpful and often perceived as being cruel. If Deming is correct that most people's performance is within three standard deviations of average, than only a very small percentage are either truly exceptional or truly poor (Deming, 1986).

How can the leader be the bearer of bad news without destroying either the output or ego of his/her employee, and how can he make performance evaluation meaningful to both parties?

No one likes to be the bearer of bad news--including leaders. That is why performance evaluation is among the greatest leadership failings. How does the servant leader deliver bad

> No one likes to be the bearer of bad news

news while demonstrating his concern for the welfare of the person being evaluated? Leaders are *not* being kind or sympathetic by *not* pointing out performance problems as these may lead to the eventual loss of the job. But it must be done in a way that the person hears and understands the problem and helps to create a plan for correction. William Rosenzweig, Managing Director of Venture Strategy Group, says truth telling is rare "because so many of us take the most well-intentioned criticism personally. The only way to unleash open communication is to convince people that honesty is about group learning, not individual criticism (Muoio, 2007). It all begins with setting the stage.

As we've said, performance evaluation should be a tool to help people grow. It is one tool, not the only tool, and it is a powerful one--if done correctly. First, we make the assumption that the leader and the employee have met prior to the start of the evaluation period and agreed upon a set of SMART goals (i.e., specific, measureable, achievable, results-oriented, and time-determined). Second, these are then measured over the evaluation period (e.g., 6 months) with a set of agreed upon metrics that are charted or otherwise displayed. Whether or not the goals are achieved can readily be ascertained with reference to the data. This method eliminates any subjective evaluation and surprises.

Major findings of years of research on performance evaluation indicate that people are most satisfied with the system when they participate in the process (DuBrin, 2003). Accordingly, Peter Drucker suggests subordinates write a "manager's letter" twice a year (Drucker, 2001). This letter is one way for subordinates to participate in the development of objectives and goals for their area of responsibility. To help people to assume a "sense of participation" or ownership, the manager's letter sets out the performance standards that the subordinate believes apply to him. Then he lists the things he must do to achieve those goals and what obstacles he must overcome within his own unit.

Jack Stack, as president and CEO, establishes standards, goals and accountabilities for about 25 people in his company. However, this is not done in isolation. "We decide *together* what expectations we'll have about their performance in the coming year, and we try to quantify as many of those as possible" (Stack, 1997, *emphasis* added).

If a goal was achieved, we ask why? Was it due to something we did, e.g., a process refinement, more experience (less time to complete a task as tasks are repeated), or just luck? If we did not achieve a goal, again we ask why? Do we need to improve the process? Was the goal unrealistically high? Did circumstances beyond our control alter the environment (e.g., Hurricane Katrina)? Or were we just unlucky? The answers to these questions may not be readily apparent and the employee should come to the evaluation with data to explain why goals were or were not achieved.

Stack takes a rather uncommon approach to goal achievement in that although he keeps a close watch on progress during the year, he restrains himself from taking any action for nine months. He says that, "I've watched too many managers stumble at first and then go on to have a great year, and it often takes three full quarters before you begin to see the results" (Stack, 1997).

Leadership Challenges for Servant Leaders

When goals are not achieved, leaders have the opportunity to teach, coach, and help employees to improve their performance. Remember to critique the work not the individual. A servant leader always has the other person's needs in mind and truly wants them to succeed. In other words, you must be clear that you are not saying "you are a bad/lazy/unskilled person," rather "that your output can be improved by doing the following ..." Nearly everyone wants to improve, develop expertise, and have a sense of satisfaction in their work. It is up to you, the leader, to create an environment where people can achieve job satisfaction and feel they are an important part of the "team."

Telling people the "bad news" is an important responsibility for leaders. You are not doing your people favors by not telling them when they are making mistakes or not working up to expectations. *How* you tell them will determine what they do about what you say. Do not be confused with a leader's responsibility to maintain discipline and the requirement to evaluate performance. Discipline problems must be addressed separately and immediately and according to a published set of rules governing conduct. For instance, a person who is frequently late to work is a discipline problem and must be handled according to organizational policy and work rules. Job performance is what we are discussing here and it is distinct from discipline.

If the leader has been measuring goal performance during the evaluation period, she should not wait until the formal evaluation to coach, teach, demonstrate, or suggest ways to improve output especially when it appears that output is not on track to achieve a goal. She should be aware, at least on a monthly basis, whether output is on, behind, or ahead of schedule and provide input to improve performance, as needed. The formal performance evaluation provides a time when

If the performance evaluation is to be effective it must be non-threatening

the two parties can sit down and discuss, analyze and evaluate goal performance. Where goals were not achieved even after frequent input from the leader, a detailed process evaluation may be called for.

If the performance evaluation is to be truly effective, it must be non-threatening. That means that discussion of pay or promotion should be done separately from this meeting. When people know that a raise or promotion is on the line, they will not be as forthcoming about their own inadequacies, lack of training or understanding. If you want the evaluation to be more than just a one-way conversation, you must divorce pay/promotion from performance (Deming, 1986).

Finally, the setting for the discussion is important. Again, it should be non-threatening. Few leaders go to the extremes that Admiral Rickover was famous for, (allegedly he sat behind a desk on a raised dais and the poor petitioner was seated in an uncomfortable chair where the two front legs had been shortened, facing him), but even subtle hints can create anxiety in the evaluatee. Both parties should be on equal ground, e.g., adjacent easy chairs, and the leader needs to begin to put the employee at ease by warmly welcoming them by name. Watch your body language so as to not send threatening signals (e.g., arms tightly crossed). Initially asking questions about family, a recent vacation or the like can help to reduce anxiety. When it appears that the person is relaxing, the evaluator should begin by asking him how *he* thinks his performance has been? Often, you will be surprised at how brutally honest people will be and much tougher on themselves than you are. After listening to their response and perhaps asking a few questions, the leader should sum up the person's performance in a few sentences. (Some like to do the summation at the end of the evaluation but doing it first tends to remove fear, especially when they hear good news!)

Leadership Challenges for Servant Leaders

Begin by telling the person something positive about their performance. Just as no one likes to hear bad things *everyone* likes to hear good things about themselves. By beginning with positive comments people will be listening to what you say. We all get defensive when confronted with criticism of our performance and some will simply stop listening if the leader begins with negative feedback. After telling them the "good" then move on to the "other."

> Just as no one likes to hear bad things, everyone likes to hear good things about themselves

When critiquing performance that is not meeting standards or goals, remember to be objective and avoid appearing to attack the individual. Demonstrate by your words and body language that you respect the person being evaluated and want the best for them. Offer suggestions and to work with the person to develop a plan for achieving their goals. Set a time to get back together again, normally within the next sixty days, to review the plan. Try to end the meeting on a high note assuring the person that you support them and want them to excel.

With proper planning, courage to tell the truth and a genuine concern for the welfare of their people, servant leaders can transform performance evaluations from something dreaded by both parties into a learning experience. Don't be surprised if you, the leader, are the real learner!

John J. Sullivan

6

Eliminate Goal-Setting?

W. Edwards Deming's 11th Point for Management reads, "Eliminate management by objective. Eliminate management by numbers, numerical goals. Substitute leadership" (Deming, 1982). Was Deming really repudiating one of Peter Drucker's most respected tools for leaders, Management by Objectives? Does this mean that goal-setting is an inappropriate leadership tool? If you don't set goals how will you measure performance?

This is a widely misunderstood teaching point. Deming expounded his 11th Point by saying that, "internal goals set in the management of a company, without a method, are burlesque" (Deming, 1982, 75). He was arguing that objectives or goals cannot be set by leaders arbitrarily and that they must first have a detailed and complete understanding of the "system" in which they are working. If that system (the process that results in the good or service of the organization) is stable (variation is within normal limits) then there is no use to specify a goal. You will get whatever the system will deliver.! To emphasize his point, he reiterates, that "To manage, one must lead. To lead, one must understand the work that he and his people are responsible for" (Deming, 1982, 76).

I don't believe that Deming meant the elimination of goal-setting as a leadership tool. What he was opposed to was the misuse and abuse of goal-setting by leaders who had little or no knowledge of the processes under study. He opposed having leaders impose unrealistic goals upon employees which often caused them to behave in unethical and even illegal ways to meet those goals.

Drucker recognized the limitations of MBO when he said, "It's just another tool. It is not the great cure for management inefficiency" (Drucker, 1982). He emphasized that managers should focus on the result, not the activity. Objectives are the basis for work and assignments but measurements for the key areas of an organization are difficult to define (Drucker, 2001). Leaders must learn to delegate tasks by assigning responsibility without assigning a detailed plan for implementation. That should be the prerogative of the one being delegated. MBO is about setting objectives and then breaking those down into more specific goals or key results.

> Drucker emphasized that managers should focus on the result, not the activity

The major principle behind MBO is to ensure that everyone within the organization has a clear understanding of the aims (objectives/goals) of the organization as well as their own roles and responsibilities in achieving those aims. According to Andy Grove, former CEO of Intel Corporation, "The one thing an MBO system should provide is focus" (Koteinikov, 2008). For MBO to be effective, individual managers must understand the specific objectives of their job and how those objectives fit in with the overall company objective set by senior leadership. "A manager's job should be based on a task to be performed in order to attain the company's objectives...the manager should be directed and controlled by the objectives of performance rather than by his boss" (Drucker, 1993).

Well then, what is the servant-first leader to do? Can she use goal-setting as a tool for performance measurement? The answer is emphatically YES! But it must be done the RIGHT way. Leaders must first realize that their people generally have the most knowledge about the processes in which they work. Leaders, even process experts, quickly lose that expertise once they are elevated to a supervisory position.

So the first step is to recognize that the person being evaluated has more knowledge about their process than the leader. They also know what is possible and what additional tools they may need to improve efficiency or expand effectiveness. Therefore the leader should first ask the employee to prepare a set of goals that promote specific objectives of their sub-organization (division, branch, office) which are, in turn, linked to the objectives of the super-organization (company, plant, church). Jack Stack,

> **Leaders must first realize that their people generally have the most knowledge about the processes in which they work.**

president and CEO of Springfield Remanufacturing Corporation, works with his senior leaders to ensure that "...these people know exactly what responsibilities and accountabilities they have for the coming year. I want the accountabilities to be very specific, at least 80% of them defined by financial ratios relating to things over which the person has total control. The final plan must not be just my plan" (Stack, 1997).

Goals must always support and promote the overall organizational goals and objectives. Their scope will be determined by the level of responsibility of the goal drafter. These are then reviewed with the leader until agreement is reached on a set of goals for the year (or quarter, month, etc.) These goals must be SMART:

- Specific

John J. Sullivan

- Measurable

- Achievable

- Results-oriented, and

- Time-determined

Specific goals are goals that can be measured. "Improve customer satisfaction," is not a measurable goal. However, "reduce the number of customer complaint calls by 15% over the next 90 days," is. Your people know what is achievable and what is not based on the resources (tools, time, technology, expertise, funds, etc.) that you as the leader have provided for them. Goals should cause people to "stretch" yet not be unrealistic and therefore demotivating. Goals should point to specific results and a time for completion. How will you know whether or not you have achieved your goal if you have not determined when the goal is to be achieved?

Let's look at some examples of well-written goals and test each one to see if they are SMART.

Goal: to increase current sales of our entire product line to Wal-Mart Stores by 15% over the next six months

Is the goal SPECIFIC? Yes, it calls for a 15% increase across the board of our product line to Wal-Mart Stores.

Is the goal MEASUREABLE? Yes, the goal is stated as 15% increase from current sales.

Is the goal ACHIEVABLE? Yes, we believe that our goal is reasonable yet will require us to "stretch." This test is based upon the best judgment of the people "in the field" and closest to the customer. But it also may include demographic or other economic studies that project an opportunity for increased sales.

Is the goal RESULTS-ORIENTED? In other words, are we looking for a *specific* result? Again, the answer is yes, the goal is very specific and calls for a *specified* increase in *current year* sales across the *entire product line* with a *specific* customer (Wal-Mart Stores).

Finally, is the goal TIME-DETERMINED? Yes, we state the goal as being achieved over the *next six months*.

Goal: increase Sunday school attendance of college and young professionals by 25% over last year's average attendance

Before we begin to dissect this goal, we need to mindful of Tuchman's (1978) caution to make clear operational definitions. We should first define the specific age group we are targeting. What ages are included in the group of "college and young professionals?" Do we only count the men and women between the ages of 18 and 29 who attend the "college and young professionals" Sunday school class? Or do we count anyone of that age group who attends any Sunday school class? What occupations will we include in the "young professionals?" What if someone is of the correct age but not in college or has a "blue collar" job? Will that person count? What constitutes "attendance?" Does someone need to attend over 50% of the classes offered? How will we determine "average attendance?" Again, we need to answer these questions ahead of time so that that there is no confusion or disagreement. Just be clear about how you will define your target market.

Leaders who treat their employees with dignity and respect will be surprised with the high standards that people will set for themselves

Leaders who treat their employees with dignity and respect and jointly enter into goal-setting as a way to measure performance, enhance productivity and focus effort, will be surprised with the high standards that people will set for themselves.

The key to successful goal-setting is highly dependent upon the attitude with which the leader approaches the process. A servant-first leader will acknowledge the expertise, dignity and maturity of his employees and treat them accordingly. Your people will surprise you with goals that truly do lead to higher productivity.

7

Strategy and Plans

Every leader of every organization should periodically do a strategic assessment; and every leader of every organization should have a strategic plan that they intend to implement or are implementing. This is equally true for servant leaders. For a new organization these may be a part of the formal business plan. For existing organizations, they form the core of long-range strategic planning and are the blueprint or template for operational planning.

I will describe a Strategic Assessment and Plan that may be utilized by any type of organization, be it a for-profit business or a not-for-profit organization. If yours is a new organization, you may find that the assessment phases 1 and 2 are most helpful. If yours is an existing organization, the assessment phases will help you identify your current state while the planning phases (3 and 4) will point you in the direction you will want to go.

The Strategic Assessment and Plan has four phases and ten steps

The Strategic Assessment and Plan has four phases and ten steps. Each of the steps has a set of questions that, taken as a whole, form the plan. The answers to the questions posed in the phases and steps provide the guidance and direction needed for sustained health and future growth. The phases are:

Phase 1: Where are we?
Phase 2: Where do we want to go?
Phase 3: How are we going to get there?
Phase 4: Are we getting there?

In this assessment phase we will determine our mission, the leader's responsibilities, and analyze the environment in which our organization exists or functions. **The first step is to determine our mission**. What is our purpose, our reason for being? Mission involves what we do now, here in the present. It may change in the future, and probably will, but at least for now, this is what we do. At this point, don't worry too much about crafting a mission statement (assuming you don't have one). That can come later. For now, focus on identifying what it is you do as an organization. Later on you can refine a succinct, coherent statement of your mission.

> Had the railroad companies recognized that they were in the business of moving people and products over long distances, today they would be vertically integrated with other means of transportation

Next we ask what *business* are we in? This requires a wide-angle view of our mission and vision for the future. For example, had the railroad companies in the 19th century recognized that they were in the business of moving people and heavy, bulky products over long distances, today they would be vertically integrated with other means of transportation to include airlines, ships, and trucks. Instead, they saw themselves as providing "rail transportation" for people and things. Others own the airlines, shipping and trucking companies. Their vision for the future was too small! Recently some friends took a trip to Alaska. The trip was booked through a vacation cruise company but involved airline transportation, rail transportation, accommodation at a luxury hotel, as well as several days spent cruising on the ship. All of these were owned by the cruise line, with the exception of the airline transportation. This is an example of a company that understands that they are in the business of providing a memorable vacation through the use of different venues and transportation mediums horizontally and vertically integrated.

Who are our customers? Our "customers" are those individuals or organizations who receive our "products" whatever they may be, past, present, and future. Who are we serving now? Who would we like to serve in the future? Determining our customer's needs will form the critical component of our future plan, i.e., how can we best meet those needs? Do we know our customer's demographics? What about lost customers? Determining why customers do not return to your organization can be difficult and time-consuming but the answers can save you future defections. And since new customers can cost up to ten times the cost of retaining existing customers, it will be money well spent (Heebsh, 2006).

> New customers can cost up to ten times the cost of retaining existing customers

Some organizations resist the concept of identifying "customers." This is especially true in education. Who *is* the customer? Is it the student, the parent, local businesses, the community? By wrestling with that question, you may find that you have several classes of customers. For example, I believe that education *does* have more than one customer. I can argue that students receive the "product" of education from faculty and staff and are therefore the "customers" of a school. At another level, I can argue that the educated student is really the "product" of that institution and the employer of its graduates is the true "customer." We can also argue that parents who fund the school (through taxes or tuition) are the true "customers" and must be satisfied. We can see that some organizations may have multiple "customers" whose needs are important and must be met in order for the organization to be successful.

The second step in Phase 1 is to identify the leader's responsibilities, leadership style and values. Ultimately, the leader is responsible for everything that the organization does or does not do. A couple of years ago a U.S. Navy nuclear submarine ran aground on an uncharted sandbar while running submerged. The captain was not at the helm yet he was held accountable and was relieved of his command when the boat returned to port. The U.S. Navy understands that the captain is ultimately responsible for the safe conduct of his vessel even when he is not physically overseeing its course; just so every organization. Does that mean that the leader should retain all responsibility unto himself and delegate nothing? Absolutely not, in fact the leader should seek to delegate all responsibilities except those few that he and he alone must do. This frees him up to concentrate on his most important tasks and creates future leaders who learn as they are delegated responsibility. Therefore, in this step we seek to identify those things that only the leader can do. The number of tasks in every organization will be small because most things can be delegated. Examples of leader-only functions might include: evaluating senior staff, administering the Sacraments, or working with senior community leaders.

Next, we examine leadership style. Don't misunderstand me, as I am not advocating abandonment of the servant-leader approach--by no means! Recent stories in the business press have highlighted companies that are apparently pulling out of a downward spiral after replacing their celebrity CEOs. Under new, low-key, people-focused leaders who seek out the counsel of their subordinates, several major corporations are effecting a turnaround. As Jim Collins discovered in researching for his book, *Good to Great*, all of the eleven "great" CEOs were self-effacing, quiet and reserved yet driven for *organizational* success (Collins, 2001). He called them Level 5 leaders; I call them servant leaders. I believe this approach to leadership, as exemplified by Jesus of Nazareth, is the best model for leading people.[3] He taught that people must be led one person at a time.

Discovering the leadership approach required of your subordinates means you must first determine each person's level of **competency** and **commitment**. Competency refers to the level of expertise and efficiency for the task assigned. Someone who has multiple tasks may have multiple levels of competency; i.e., they may be very good at one task but less so at another. Evaluation of competency is *task-specific*. The degree of leader involvement is dependent upon the *task* and not the individual. In other words, you may need to be more involved in coaching and guiding someone who has low competency with a specific task but have little direct involvement with other tasks where their competency level is high.

> Discovering the leadership approach required of your subordinates means you must first determine each person's level of competency and commitment

Organizational commitment is *global* in nature. That is, ones level of commitment to the success of the organization is not dependent upon a specific task. The leader's challenge with this type of person is to move them from an "enrolled" status to one of commitment. A person who is merely enrolled is one who does what is required, nothing more, nothing less. She has no long-term interest in the organization and displays little or no loyalty. On the other hand, a person who is truly committed to an organization takes the initiative to do what needs to be done for the organization

---

[3] For a complete discussion of Jesus as leader see the author's book, *Servant First! Leadership for the New Millennium*, Xulon Press, 2004.

to be successful. She does not wait to be told her job, she seeks out ways to improve, refine, and build quality and efficiency.

Leaders should examine their staff and seek to discover each person's level of competency and commitment and then decide the level of leader involvement and delegated responsibility appropriate to each. This does not mean foregoing an overall servant-leader approach. It does mean that you will be more involved on a daily basis with some employees and less with others.

The final substep involves a comparison of organizational values and the leader's personal values. Are the two in agreement? If not, then the leader must take some action to either change the culture of the organization or his personal values. In an entrepreneurial start-up, organizational values generally reflect the leader's values. In an existing organization, the inherited values of an organization may have changed over its lifespan and are no longer healthy to growth. This can frequently happen as an organization becomes larger and begins to take on the negative qualities of a bureaucracy (not that *all* bureaucratic characteristics are negative). For example, with the introduction of competition in the telecommunication industry, telephone companies who formerly operated a monopoly are now faced with a new model for customer service. Those companies who will consistently provide superior customer service at a fair price will be successful. Others who do not treat customers as assets will not survive.

The third and final step in Phase 1 is to analyze the environments in which an organization exists, internally and externally. This is often referred to as SWOT analysis: strengths and weaknesses (internally), and opportunities and threats (externally). What are our own organizational strengths? What are our distinctive competencies and our competitive advantage, i.e., what sets

What are our distinctive competencies and our competitive advantage?

68

us apart from others that have the same or similar mission? For a business, this means asking why should a customer do business with us over one of our competitors? For a non-profit, such as a church, it means asking why should a family attend our church rather than another church closer to home? An organization that cannot identify its competitive advantage is doomed to failure. So if you don't know what your competitive advantage is, you might as well get out of business now and save yourself the headaches of certain failure in the future. But it may also include: location, availability and education of the workforce, cost control, quality level, worker satisfaction, use of technology and the like. What are our weaknesses? These may include many of the same categories listed under strengths. We must be brutally honest here and seek to build on our strengths and mitigate our weaknesses.

As we look to the external environment, we identify our competitors and not only those who offer a similar product but also those who have a product that may be substituted for ours. For example, a company operating a golf driving range and batting cages needs to look beyond other driving ranges/batting cages and consider companies offering recreation services as potential competitors. What are the strengths and weaknesses of our competitors? Consider factors such as: location, level of technology, prices, reputation, longevity, community involvement, and customer service. What are the barriers to entry to our business/industry? What are the opportunities and threats in the external environment? Is the local government a threat or an opportunity? Companies operating internationally will consider this as one of the major environmental factors. Consider other factors such as: number of competitors, regulations, environmental constraints, natural resources, transportation infrastructure and the state of the economy.

Once we have done a thorough assessment of our current condition, we turn to the question of what do we want to become?

Here we look to the future by working through the next four steps to develop our vision and organizational values; identify key processes and systems; determine gaps in performance; and finally, establish objectives and goals.

You will recall that in Phase 1 we developed our mission, i.e., our purpose, our reason for being. Mission is what we do NOW; it is oriented to the present. Vision is what we hope to do in the future. It is a unifying picture of where the organization is going and enables everyone to focus on the same distant point on the horizon. Our mission may change as we move toward our vision over time

> The proof that we have the vision is that we are reaching out for more than we have grasped.
> --Oswald Chambers

but our vision should remain. Mission and vision form two elements of the organization's Guiding Principles. The third element is values, which will be discussed below (Sullivan, 2004).

Step 4 is development of the organizational vision and values. That vision should be a *shared vision*. It will not be effective as a guiding principle if it is only the leader's vision. The leader has an important role to play in visioning but his role cannot be as the sole author and enforcer of the vision. A vision statement crafted by a leader or even an executive group without input and critique from the people within the organization will not become a shared vision. Sorry, it just won't happen. So how do we achieve a shared vision?

Servant leaders know that people are more committed to decisions when they have been involved in the decision process. Even if an individual's opinions and ideas are not accepted along the path to a final decision, the fact that you listened to them and considered their input is vital to their commitment to implementation. Therefore it is important that as many people as possible in the organization have an opportunity to provide input on the organizational vision statement. Practically, how do you do that?

Here is where the leader comes in because without the leader's active involvement there will be no vision. (See Proverbs 29:18) The leader must *initiate* the discussion of a vision of a future state, an organization that we hope to become. She may even have a small group of people draft a vision statement after talking to as many people in the organization as possible about what they see in the future for our organization. Once this is done, I like Stephen Covey's recommendation to send the statement out with an invitation to critique it that reads something like this: *"Here is the draft vision statement. We don't much like it either so we'd like to hear from you!"* (Covey, 1989). That gives license to tear it apart. If you don't do that then it becomes the "boss' vision statement" and your people will be fearful to openly criticize it. Your only input will be laudatory comments that do nothing to create commitment to the vision.

The third element in our organizational Guiding Principles is values, i.e., how will we treat each other and our "customers" (those we serve) on our way toward our vision? In the first phase, we discussed the leader's values and how they must examine their own set of values and how they relate to the organization. In this step, we are determining what those organizational values currently are, or if this is a new organization, what we want them to be. Organizational values that form and shape the organizational culture are often unspoken but are simply "the way we do things around here." A new leader coming in to an existing organization may be surprised to learn the dominant values practiced in the organization. What is down on paper and the "way things really work" may be two entirely

> Organizational values that form and shape the organizational culture are simply "the way we do things around here"

different things. Ask lots of questions and values will emerge. It may take setting up a series of scenarios: if this happens, how do we deal with it? For example: What do we tell a customer when a shipment will be late especially if he represents a large percentage of our total sales?

How are we going to treat each other *within* the organization? What level of trust are we comfortable with? For example, an organization that trusts and respects its employees will not hesitate to share its financial details. The company is saying, in effect: *we trust you and respect your judgment and opinions such that we are willing to disclose our most intimate financial details with you since this is your company too!* However, you must live out those values for them to become truly a part of the culture. Southwest Airlines is famous for its customer service. They live out their value of putting customers' needs first. However, if the day arrives where an employee is disciplined for taking too much time with a customer that value dies. The old value is replaced with "speed = profit" and the needs of customers move to the back of the line. So be careful what you say you value because your people will be watching to see if you really mean it.

Step 5 is to identify your key processes and systems. What are the few key systems and processes that differentiate us from our competitors and give us competitive advantage? Most organizations do lots of things but there are a few, select systems and processes that set the organization apart from others that are critical. We must do these well or we will not survive as an organization. The great football coach Vince Lombardi was very successful, in part, because he focused on the essentials: tackling and blocking. What is essential to the success of your organization? What are those systems and processes that are most important to its survival? For example, a liberal arts college must provide good, sound classroom instruction in order to survive. They do lots of other things but classroom instruction is critical to the future of the organization. Likewise, the manufacturing processes of an automobile maker are critical to its success. If they don't build a quality automobile, all the glib marketing in the world won't save it from ruin. For a church, the Sunday worship service is a critical system or series of processes involving facilities, music, prayers, scripture reading, a message preached, and the coordination of a host of people. A beautiful campus or an award-winning day care facility will not keep the doors of that church open; focusing on the critical systems will.

Step 6 is to determine the gaps in performance in our key systems and processes. We do this because we know that these systems and processes are essential to our survival and we must do them well. The Pareto Principle states that 80% of consequences stem from 20% of the causes (Reh, 2006). Therefore we should focus on those few essential systems and processes, as they will impact most of the other systems within the organization. First, we must gather data on our current level of performance in our key systems and processes. The metrics we choose are also critical since we must find what truly measures our *effectiveness* and that can take some time and trial. For example, the number of hours an employee spends in professional growth seminars is *not* a good metric for their level of training. What the person is able to *do* with the new knowledge is what you want to measure. Finding a metric that does that is the challenge.

Once we feel that we have a good understanding of the steady state performance of our key systems, then we compare that condition with our desired future state. How do we determine what the standard should be? One way is to look to those organizations in whatever industry that consistently produce world-class results in a given area or system. If you were to stop by the L.L. Bean headquarters in Freeport, Maine, today you would see people from all over the world who are not there to purchase items from the L.L. Bean retail store—although they may indulge a bit. They are there to learn how L.L. Bean is able to produce, market, and ship their many products all over the world with great efficiency, accuracy and timeliness. L.L. Bean *is* the world standard and thankfully they are willing to share their expertise with others.

As we compare our key processes and systems against such standards, are there gaps in performance? In most cases, there will be. Now our task is to develop objectives and goals to close those gaps.

Step 7, the final step in Phase 2, is where we establish strategic and operational objectives that once obtained, will close the gaps in performance in our key systems and processes. The terms "objectives" and "goals" are sometimes interchanged but I prefer to use the term objective to mean an over-arching or super-goal and goals as a series of measurable targets leading up to an objective. *Strategic* objectives are those longer-term objectives that will take 3-5 years to complete. That is the time frame generally accepted as long-term, at least in the West. Eastern cultures tend to think in much long terms as witnessed by Konosuke Matsushita, founder and CEO of Matsushita Electric, the global Japanese electronics firm, who some years ago asked his senior executives to think 250 years out (Clawson, 2006). Jesus' challenge to "... go make disciples of all the nations, baptizing them in the name of the Father and the Son and the Holy Spirit," (Matthew 29:19) is a strategic objective many centuries out!

Operational objectives are to be completed within a year. An example of a strategic objective for a manufacturing company might be to **develop new product lines for Eastern Europe**. An operational objective supporting this could be to **develop and market one new product for Eastern Europe.** A strategic objective for an urban church could be to **establish a youth drop-in center for teens** or **develop and implement parenting skills training for single parents**.

Goals then are established under each objective that leads to completion of at least one element of that objective. These goals must be SMART: specific, measurable, achievable, results-oriented, and time-determined. For example:

Strategic Objective: Develop new product lines for Eastern Europe
Goal: Within 90 days, determine customer needs for our products and available suppliers within Eastern Germany

Specific: determine needs and suppliers within Eastern Germany
Measurable: listing of expressed product needs and outlets for supply
Achievable: we believe this can be done in the time allotted
Results-oriented: specific results have been identified
Time-determined: complete within three months

Strategic Objective: Establish a youth drop-in center for teens
Goal: By January 1, create a prioritized listing of available suitable existing buildings listed under $500,000 within 3 miles of church

Specific: determine inventory of available, suitable building near our facility
Measurable: physical count of buildings meeting our criteria
Achievable: we believe this can be done in the time allotted
Results-oriented: specific results have been identified
Time-determined: a deadline has been established

Each objective may have several goals. The more complex the objective the more goals we can expect. Objectives must support the mission and vision of the organization. Likewise, goals will support one or more objectives. Objectives that are not directly tied to furthering the organization's mission and vision should not be considered.

This phase, which has a single step, requires the development of an implementation plan and systems for monitoring performance.

Step 8 involves development of an implementation plan for the objectives and goals determined in Phase 2. Remember that each objective and its associated goal(s) are carefully selected to close a measurable gap between our current level of performance in key systems and processes and the desired future state. For each goal, we must determine:

- Who will be assigned responsibility for completion of the goal?
- What steps are to be accomplished?
- What resources will be made available?
- How should the work be accomplished?
- When do we want the goal completed?

Who will be held responsible for accomplishing the goal? This involves *delegation* of responsibility from a leader to a subordinate. This must be done since a task cannot simply be assigned to a group of people with the expectation that they will accept the responsibility and accomplish the task. Some*one* must be held directly responsible.

Successful delegation involves three elements: *responsibility*, *authority* and *accountability*. When a leader assigns *responsibility* for a task to a subordinate, he is, in effect, transferring *his* responsibility to that person. As discussed in Phase 1, the leader is responsible for everything the organization does or does not do. But he can and must delegate direct responsibility for tasks to subordinates. In order for the person to effectively accomplish the task assigned, he must also receive the *authority* to call upon resources needed to accomplish the goal. Those resources may include people, material, technology, funds, equipment, time, or whatever is needed to get the job done. Finally, the person assigned will be held accountable for accomplishment of the task. Failure to perform a delegated task successfully is usually attributable to the leader's failure at delegating one of the essential elements. Often, that element is authority.

The Gospels record Jesus delegating responsibility to His disciples as He prepared them to assume leadership: "... Jesus called together his twelve apostles and gave them *power* and *authority* to cast out demons and to heal all diseases. Then he sent them out to tell everyone about the coming of the Kingdom of God and to heal the sick" (*emphasis* added. Luke 9:1,2). When He had finished delegating these responsibilities, Jesus "... went off teaching and preaching in towns throughout the country" (Matthew 11:1). Not long after delegating authority to heal and exorcise, we see evidence that Jesus delegated other leadership responsibilities to his disciples in the feeding of the five thousand. Confronted with their plea to "send the crowds away to the nearby villages and farms, so they can find food and lodging for the night," (Matthew 9:12), Jesus turns to the disciples and commands, "*You* feed them," (*emphasis* added. Matthew 9:13). Jesus has made clear to these His future leaders that He has delegated not only the *responsibility* to care for the people but also the *authority* to call upon resources to successfully complete each task.

> Failure to perform a delegated task successfully is usually attributable to the leader's failure at delegating one of the essential elements

The steps to be accomplished are a series of events that must be completed in order for the goal to be realized. At this level they should be generalized while leaving the details to the person assigned and their team to determine. The same principle applies to the question of how should the work be accomplished. Leave the details to the leader and their team to determine how best to accomplish the steps.

The resources needed to accomplish the task must be authorized or assigned by the senior leader whenever they exceed the normal level of authority of the delegated leader. This is best done in writing and formal notice given to other senior leaders in the organization of the delegated leader's authority and the duration of the task. This is especially important when people from another part of the organization may be required to assist in task accomplishment.

Assigning a date/time for goal accomplishment makes very clear to all when the job must be completed. If follow on tasks will depend upon completion of the task assigned, the person assigned and their team should also know this.

One way to display goals is with a grid, as depicted in Table 1, below.

Table 1

GOAL	WHO?	STEPS	RESOURCES	HOW?	WHEN?
Determine customer needs in E. Germany	Roger Smith's team in marketing	1. Survey potential customers 2. Determine substitutes 3. Identify brand loyalty	1. Smith's team of 4 2. Direct mailing up to 20,000 homes 3. Funds necessary for analytic reporting by contractor	1. By random survey 2. Suppliers within E. Germany 3. Buyers for major retail chains	Final report by 15 July
Determine suitable space for youth center	Jim Brown, Youth Minister	1. Determine our youth population over next 15 years 2. Determine square footage and facilities needed 3. Identify available structures w/i 3 mile radius	1. Brown + Facility Director 2. Church Realty Division 3. Church sedan	1. Review projected demographic growth in youth pop 2. Survey youth & other churches with youth centers for needs 3. Major realtors for buildings availability 4. Prioritized list of buildings under $500K	Preliminary report by 1 Dec; final report by 1 Jan

Leadership Challenges for Servant Leaders

Critical to the success of the implementation plan is the integration of the overall strategic plan with operational plans, and their associated budgets, and personnel evaluation. This insures that operational plans and goals flow from and directly support the strategic plan and that subordinate leaders are evaluated based on the results of goal accomplishment.

Finally we turn to the fourth phase where we will establish a review process for changing our strategic direction and ensuring that our plan stays fresh and relevant over time.

These two last steps involve monitoring performance, analyzing feedback, review and evaluation. This is the phase most often overlooked or underappreciated but critical to the success of our strategic plan. is an old but true proverb. Therefore, as discussed in Step 6, our choice of metrics is vitally important to goal achievement. Do we measure *effectiveness*, i.e., doing the right things, or *efficiency*, i.e., doing things right? **Step 9, therefore, is where we determine how we will measure objective/goal accomplishment and identify other means for progress feedback**. This

> What gets measured gets done

step is often overlooked because it is difficult and frequently frustrating to determine the measures that will tell you what you need to know. The fast and easy choices often don't measure our true success or failure. Finding the right metrics can be a process of trial and error. That's why it is necessary to frequently review and evaluate the data and its associated metric. For example, does counting the number of conferences or workshops attended tell us whether or not a leader understands and can apply servant leadership to his everyday responsibilities? How do we measure the *results* of his education?

Normally, leaders will want to use more than one metric to gain a true perspective on goal accomplishment. Selecting a quantitative *and* a qualitative metric may provide more realistic feedback than simply relying on a quantitative measurement alone.

79

For example, measuring customer satisfaction with a product by tracking the number of complaints received for that product may only tell us part of the story. Talking with customers may reveal that problems with the product have caused customer defections to competing products. The customers are not complaining because they are no longer your customers!

Jesus was debating with some teachers of religious law when one of the men spoke up to say that his son was mute and possessed by an evil spirit, which caused him to have violent seizures. He had taken the boy to Jesus' disciples for healing but they were unable to cast out the evil spirit. When the lad was brought forward, Jesus rebuked the spirit, healed him, and sent father and son happily on their way. Later, His disciples questioned Him as to why they could not cast out the evil spirit. Jesus replied, "This kind can be cast out only by prayer," (Mark 9:14-29). Jesus used feedback from a "customer" to measure the effectiveness of His delegation of responsibility and authority to cast out evil spirits and to heal. He held His disciples responsible for performing the work and when presented with evidence that they were not completely successful, He corrected them and sent them out again.

Step 10 is review and evaluation. Here we determine the process for continued review of our progress on objective/goal accomplishment. How frequently will we review the data? What level of variation (deviation from plan) will cause us to change our implementation plan? What criteria will we use for changing strategic direction? How often will we review our mission and vision? What events would cause us to change? These questions need to be answered with broad participation throughout the organization. I recommend that the senior level of the organization conduct an annual review of its Guiding Principles and its major objectives. Objectives and associated goals should be reviewed at least semiannually at the division level and more frequently (quarterly/monthly) at the next level down.

Dr. Dan Struble, President of Montreat College, insures that the strategic planning process continues throughout the year by holding quarterly MIT (monitoring and implementation team) meetings to evaluate progress, assess changes in the environment and shift priorities, resources and initiatives to reflect the dynamic environment within which the organization operates.

The Ritz-Carlton Hotel chain, long the leader in the luxury hotel sector, recently conducted just such a review. Recognizing the changing demographics in the typical high-end hotel guest, the "name that has defined luxury as a cross between formal elegance and unwavering service" (Sanders 2006, B1) has announced that they are abandoning their 20 rules for dealing with guest requests and adopting instead 12 service values. Rather than adhering to a rigid set of responses for each situation, According to the president and chief executive officer, Simon Cooper, hotel chains in this sector are struggling with how to define luxury in a crowded and evolving market. The typical luxury hotel traveler is no longer necessarily a middle-age male businessman or a wealthy jet-setter but could be a 30-something in a T-shirt and jeans. This new type of guest often doesn't want to be addressed in the old, more formal way. This has caused a reassessment at the very core of what the company stands for. Vivian Deuschl, vice president for public relations, affirmed that the Ritz is not changing their values, rather they are freeing their associates to better meet the needs of guests while maintaining high standards for service (V. Deuschl, personal communication, June 29, 2006). This type of assessment and targeted response to environmental changes are what keep companies like the Ritz-Carlton at the top of their industry.

The "ladies and gentlemen" of the Ritz-Carlton chain will be asked to think for themselves

John J. Sullivan

Appendix A

The Strategic Assessment and Plan
An Outline

Phase 1: Where are we?

1. Determine the mission
   - What is our purpose, reason for existence?
   - What business are we in?
   - Who are our customers?
2. Identify the leader's responsibilities, leadership style & values
   - What are the things only the leader can do? (i.e., what *cannot* be delegated?)
   - What leadership style is required given the circumstances (level of commitment & competency)?
   - How will the leader's own personal values affect the organization?
3. Analyze the external & internal environments
   - What are our own internal strengths & weaknesses?
   - What are our distinctive competencies/competitive advantages?
   - Who are our competitors & what are their strengths & weaknesses?
   - What other external threats & opportunities can we identify?

Phase 2: Where do we want to go?

4. Develop the organizational vision & values
   - What is our vision for the future of our organization?

- What values will we adhere to in dealing with our customers (those we serve), both external & internal?

5. Identify key processes & systems
   - What are the few, key systems & processes that differentiate us from our competitors?
   - What are those systems & processes that are most important to our survival?

6. Determine gaps in performance
   - What is our current level of performance in our key systems & processes?
   - When we compare our current performance with our desired future state, are there gaps in systems or processes?

7. Establish objectives & goals
   - What are the strategic and operational objectives that, once obtained, will close our gaps in performance?
   - What are the necessary goals we will need to achieve in order to accomplish our stated objectives?

Phase 3: How are we going to get there?

8. Develop the implementation plan

For each goal, determine:
   - Who will be assigned responsibility?
   - What steps are to be accomplished?
   - What resources are available?
   - How will the work be accomplished (in general terms)?
   - When do we want the goal completed?

Phase 4: Are we getting there?

9. Monitor performance & feedback analysis
   - How will we measure goal accomplishment?
   - What other means will we use for feedback on our progress?

10. Review & evaluation

Leadership Challenges for Servant Leaders

- What will be the process for continual review of our progress?
- What criteria will we use for changing strategic direction?

John J. Sullivan

References

Barkman, D., (1997), *Open-book Management, Your EZ Intro to OBM*, Knoxville, TN: The Business Center.

Boom, C., (1973), *The Hiding Place*, Boston: G.K. Hall

Burlingham, B., (1989), "Being the Boss," *Inc. Magazine*, October 1989.

Case, J., (1998), *The Open-Book Experience, Lessons from Over 100 Companies Who Successfully Transformed Themselves*, Reading, MA: Perseus Books.

Kendall, R.T., (2002), *Total Forgiveness*, Lake Mary, FL: Charisma House

Clawson, J., (2006). Personal and Organizational Charters. http://faculty.darden.virginia.edu/clawsonj/pdf/ClawCh12v2_072205.pdf (July 8, 2006)

Collins, J.C., (2001). *Good to Great: Why Some Companies Make the Leap...and Others Don't*. New York, NY: HarperCollins Publishers, Inc.

Covey, S.R., (1989). *The 7 Habits of Highly Effective People: Powerful Lessons in Personal Change*. New York, NY: Simon & Schuster, Inc.

Deming, W., (1986), *Out of the Crisis*, Cambridge, MA: MIT

Drucker, P., (1982), *The Practice of Management*, New York: HarperCollins

Drucker, P., (1993), *Management: Tasks, Responsibilities, Practices*, New York: HarperCollins

Drucker, P., (2001), *The Essential Drucker*, New York: HarperCollins

DuBrin, A., (2003), *Essentials of Management, Sixth Edition*, Mason, OH: South-Western

Ford, L., (1991), *Transforming Leadership, Jesus' Way of Creating Vision, Shaping Values & Empowering Change*, Downers Grove, IL: InterVarsity Press

Greenleaf, R.K., (1991), *Servant Leadership, A Journey into the Nature of Legitimate Power and Greatness*, Mahwah, NJ: Paulist Press

Heebsh, A., (2006). "Customers: the new window to profitability." *Teradata Magazine*. http://www.teradata.com/t/page/135376/index.html (June 29, 2006).

Koteinikov, V. (2008), "Management by Objectives (MBO)," 1000ventures.com, http:www.1000ventures.com/business_guide/mgmt_mbo_main.html (7/18/2008)

Mathis, R. and Jackson, J., (1999), *Human Resource Management*, Cincinnati, OH: South-Western College Publishing

Muoio, A., (2007), *The Truth Is, the Truth Hurts*, FastCompany.com, http://www.fastcompany.com/magazine/14/one.html, accessed May 15, 2008

Leadership Challenges for Servant Leaders

"Open-Book Management and Corporate Performance," The National Center for Employee Ownership, http://www.nceo.org/library/obm_nceostudy.html (4/23/2008)

Reh, F.J. Pareto's Principle-The 80-20 Rule. About Management. http://management.about.com/cs/generalmanagement/a/Pareto081202.htm (June 28, 2006).

Sandberg, J, (2006), *The Wall Street Journal*, April 25, 2006, B1

Sanders, P., (2006). "Taking' Off the Ritz—a Tad." *Wall Street Journal*, June 23, 2006, B1.

Scholtes, P.R., Joiner, B.L., and Streibel, B.J. (1996*), The Team Handbook, Second Edition*, Madison, WI: Joiner Associates, Inc.

Stack, J. (1994), *The Great Game of Business*, New York: Doubleday "The Case for Open-Book Management, Winning Workplaces, http://www.the fabricator.com/CEOs/CEOs_Article.cfm?ID=960 (4/23/2008)

Stack, J. (1997), "The Curse of the Annual Performance Review," *Inc. Magazine*, March 1997

Sullivan, J.J., (2004). *Servant First! Leadership for the New Millennium*. Longwood, FL: Xulon Press.

Tuckman, B., (1978). *Conducting Educational Research*. New York: Harcourt, Brace, Jovanovich

Walton, M., (1990), *Deming Management at Work*, New York: Putnam

White, E., (2007), *The Wall Street Journal*, Managing, August 13, 2007, B1

89

John J. Sullivan

About the Author

John J. Sullivan is the director of ServantLeader Ministries whose mission is to educate, encourage and equip leaders in all walks of life who desire to serve rather than be served.

He has had a wide variety of career experiences. He has served as a Marine Corps fighter pilot, a squadron and air station commander, senior staff officer, consultant, quality examiner, athletics director, professor, and conference commissioner. He is widely acclaimed as an authority on servant leadership as an author, a teacher and a practitioner.

A highly decorated Vietnam veteran, prior to entering academia he served for 28 years in the U.S. Marine Corps as a helicopter gunship pilot, fighter pilot, squadron commander, senior staff officer, base commander, and professor, retiring as a colonel. As a senior staff officer in the Pentagon, he was Program Coordinator for what was then the Department of the Navy's largest development and acquisition program, the F/A-18 Hornet aircraft. While he was the Commanding Officer, Marine Corps Air Station Beaufort, SC, the base was selected in worldwide competition as the best installation in the Marine Corps and received the prestigious Commander-in-Chief's Award for Installation Excellence.

He was the Course Director of Policy Making and Implementation within the National Security Decision Making Department and professor of management at the Naval War College, Newport, RI. He taught in the graduate program primarily in leadership education.

An American Society for Quality Certified Quality Manager, he was a founder of the Rhode Island Area Coalition for Excellence (RACE),

John J. Sullivan

helped design its State quality award, and was its first lead examiner.

Following his military career, Sullivan served for nine years as an associate professor of business at Montreat College, Montreat, NC. His teaching focus was in the disciplines of leadership and management.

He is a graduate of the University of Southern California, Webster University and the Naval War College.

Visit http://www.servantleaderministries.org for more information on servant leadership or the author.